SETH RIGGS

SINGING FOR THE STARS

A Complete Program for Training Your Voice

Compiled and Edited by
John Dominick Carratello

Revised Edition

From Signor Mufti of the original Schola Cantorum, to his pupil Riccardo Daviesi, to his pupil E. Herbert-Caesare; on to Antonio Cotogni, to Mattia Battistini, to Benjamino Gigli, to my early teachers John Charles Thomas, Robert Weede, Tito Schipa and Helge Rösevenge my eternal gratitude for vocal direction; this particular vocal pedagogy and tradition is the one I've tried to follow, explore and emulate.

A very special thanks to my editor, John Dominick Carratello. Without John, this book would probably never have been written. Together, we wanted to formulate and develop a book such as this—a book about singing that could be understood and used by everyone, professional and amateur alike. John skillfully synthesized and structured the information he got from observing me at work, and from our many hours of discussion. His own background and knowledge of the subject was, of course, invaluable. The results of his thoroughness in presenting my approach will be apparent to the reader.

Seth Riggs

CONTENTS

Foreword 5

Preface 7

Acknowledgments 8

About the Author 9

Introduction 12

How To Use This Book 19

Basic Principles 21

How Your Voice Works
The Creation of Vocal Tone 21

Vocal Cord Vibration—
Where Your Voice Begins 22

Breath support 24

Vocal cord adjustment 27

Resonance—Why Your Voice Is Unique 29

Physical sensations 30

What to Remember 30

How Your Voice Works Best
The Natural Technique of Speech-Level Singing . .31

Your Speech-Level—
A Foundation for Vocal Freedom 31

Speech-level Singing—
Feeling and Sounding Natural 34

Singing low notes 34

Singing high notes 34

The passage areas of your range 35

Singing through the passage areas 35

Vocal cord thinning 37

Vocal cord shortening 37

What to Remember 37

How to Get Your Voice to Work for You
The Training Process 38

Developing Coordination—
The First Step 38

Building Strength—All in Good Time 39

What to Remember 39

Practical Exercises 40

Part 1
Building Confidence 41

Exercise 1 42

Exercise 2 43

Exercise 3 44

Exercise 4 44

Exercise 5 46

Exercise 6 46

Exercise 7 48

Exercise 8 49

Exercise 9 50

Exercise 10 51

Exercise 11 52

Exercise 12 54

Exercise 13 55

Part 2
Toward Speech-Level Singing 57

Exercise 14 58

Exercise 15 59

Exercise 16 60

Exercise 17 61

Exercise 18 62

Exercise 19 63

Exercise 20 64

Exercise 21 65

Exercise 22 66

Exercise 23 67

Exercise 24 68

Exercise 25 69

Exercise 26 70

Part 3
Technique Maintenance 71

Exercise 27 72

Exercise 28 73

Exercise 29 74

Exercise 30 75

The Author Speaks Out 76

    General Questions 76

    Classifying Voices 76

    Range Extension 76

    Tone Development 78

    Using Microphones 78

    Singing in Different Styles 78

    Singing Outdoors 78

    Choosing a Teacher .79

    Exploiting Student Voices 79

    Voice Science 79

    Performers as Teachers 80

    Singing in Choir 80

    Choir Directors as Voice Teachers 81

    Popular Music and Traditional Teaching 81

    Selecting Music 82

    Singing in Foreign Languages 82

    Practicing 83

    Singing in Rehearsals 84

    Voice Competitions .84

    The Young Voice 84

    The Aging Voice 85

Health and Care of the Singer's Voice 86

    Your Posture 86

    Bad Habits 86

        Using alcohol and drugs 86

        Smoking 86

        Eating before singing 86

        Shocking your cords 87

        Using excessive volume 87

    Other Factors 87

        Imitation of other singers 87

        Remedies that don't work 87

        Unnecessary vocal rest 87

        Emotional stress and fatigue 87

        Hormones 87

        Your environment 87

Appendix 88

Glossary 91

Compact Disc Index 95

FOREWORD

The wide diversity of singing styles that exists in the world today demands a singing technique—a way of using your voice—that can be applied in the performance of all those styles. If a singing technique can't be applied to *every* style of singing, something is wrong with that technique.

That's the premise we began with when Alfred Publishing Company's editors and I discussed the development of a totally new kind of book about singing. We wanted to do something that had never been done before—publish a book that actually taught people *how* to sing.

But where would we find the author? There was only one person I knew of who could fill such a tall order—Seth Riggs, considered by many to be the best and most successful voice teacher in the United States. He is certainly the busiest. No other teacher, past or present, has ever matched his phenomenal track record. His students are a veritable "Who's Who" of singers, actors, dancers, and entertainers throughout the world.*

When you first meet Seth Riggs, you are overwhelmed by his dynamic personality, his flair for the outspoken, but most of all, his sense of purpose— his "mission" to clean up the mess being made of singers' voices by voice teachers in schools, colleges, and private studios everywhere.

The day I met with Seth about the possibility of putting his method in writing so more people could benefit from his work, his initial reaction was, "Impossible—you can't learn to sing from a book!" Well, I could understand his point of view. When Seth Riggs teaches, it's strictly on a one-to-one basis. He quickly diagnoses a singer's vocal problems and then prescribes specific exercises to correct those problems. It's a very individual process, one not easily adapted to the printed page. But we decided to give it a try. It *had* to be done.

I proceeded to do my research and to observe him closely over a period of several months, trying to find a general or systematic approach to something that, there was no question about it, was working miracles!

*See Appendix for a listing of his clientele on page 88.

The first time I sat in on a lesson, I thought I had gone to singers' heaven! Seth had his students doing incredible things with their voices— things you would have thought only those with a great natural gift could do. In the weeks that followed, most of the students I observed weren't even part of the "star" clientele he has become so famous for. But they *sounded* like stars.

Like so many others, these singers—young and old—had struggled unsuccessfully for years with other "voice teachers" to increase their range and improve their tone quality. With Seth Riggs, however, the results were very different, and achieved in a very short time. You see, the Riggs method is application. Although he likes his students to understand the basic principles underlying his method, he feels that just telling you how your voice works does nothing to help you sing. You have to know how to get it to work

Well, finally the "impossible" had been accomplished. The manuscript was complete, as well as a CD that actually demonstrates how to do the exercises used in the training program. Yet, something wasn't right. Oh, it was all there—the theory, the exercises, all the facts. But that special quality of the man you experience between the actual moments of instruction— his charisma, if you like—was missing.

To remedy this, we included a section entitled "The Author Speaks Out," in which Seth talks more informally about his method and responds very frankly (that is his way) to the controversial issues surrounding the teaching of singing in this country and abroad.

I am confident that readers of this book will appreciate and utilize its direct, no-nonsense approach to developing a workable vocal technique— to begin *Singing for the Stars*.

The Editor

"Sing from your diaphragm!" "Place the tone forward!" "Open your throat!" "Keep your tongue down!" "Give it more support!" Sound familiar?

The language of voice teachers and choir directors abounds in such confusing and dangerous cliches. Every day, singers who never question the "wisdom" of their teachers manipulate and strain their voices until one day they discover their voices are "burned out."

What most teachers never seem to understand is that you don't need to think about twenty different things every time you open your mouth. And you don't need to study singing for more than a few weeks before you begin to experience positive results.

It doesn't matter whether you sing pop, rock, opera, or musical theatre. You should sing with a technique that allows you to just relax and concentrate on performing—which is what it's really all about, anyway—right?

This author has worked successfully with hundreds of singers, actors, and dancers—top professionals—in all areas of musical performance and entertainment. And although some may not sing as well as others, all have achieved the ability to always sound confident and natural when they sing.

Their secret is a technique called speech-level singing, which allows you to sing with the same comfortable, easily produced voice you use, or should use, when you speak. No matter if you sing high or low, loud or soft, nothing feels different in your throat or mouth. Your tone and the words you sing always feel natural to you, and sound natural to your audience.

With this book and the accompanying CDs, you can now learn the same singing technique the pros use—one that will let you sing with a strong, clear, and flexible voice over a range that you never dreamed possible. But it does take patience and the ability to follow instructions carefully.

Good luck! I wish you all the success in the world.

Seth Riggs

ACKNOWLEDGMENTS

The following teachers are certified and accredited by Seth Riggs to apply the Speech-Level Singing technique. Teachers without proper licensing are not considered valid.

Randy Buescher—Chicago & Napville, IL

Sandy Cressman—San Francisco, CA

Rodj Dullapan—Bangkok, Thailand

Lorna Emata—San Jose, CA

Gregory Enriquez—Las Vegas, NV

Mary Beth Felker—Portland, OR

Joy Fields—Maui, HI

Jennifer Winters Goodrich—Sherman Oaks, CA

Michael Goodrich—Sherman Oaks, CA

Rocio Guitard—San Francisco, CA

Katie Guthorn—San Francisco, CA

Dean Kaelin—Salt Lake City, UT

Dolly Kanekuni—Kauai, HI

Kathy Kennedy—San Francisco & Berkeley, CA

Deborah Levoy—San Jose, CA

Badiene Magaziner—NYC & Cherry Hill, NJ

Brett Manning—Nashville, TN

Daria Mautner—San Francisco & Novato, CA

Judith May—San Francisco, CA

Tom McKinney—Houston, TX

Leigh McRae—Sydney, Australia

Vanessa Purdy—Phoenix, AZ

Rachel Rains—Nashville, TN

David Romano—Los Angeles, CA

Betty Schneider—Berkeley, CA

Jodi Sellars—Van Nuys, CA

Cary Sheldon—Berkeley, CA

Jeffrey Skouson—Las Vegas, NV

Lani Stark—Honokaa, HI

Dave Stroud—Phoenix, AZ and San Francisco
    & Sacramento, CA

Saburo Takada—Tokyo, Japan

Mary Walkley—Miami & Tampa Bay, FL

Spencer Welch—Surrey, BC

Whendae—Los Angeles, CA

Kim Woods—Nashville, TN

Additionally, the author acknowledges the following individuals:

Richard Miller, the most inspirational pedagogue I've ever met.

Dr. Henry Rubin (deceased), Dr. Edward Kantor, Dr. Hans Von Leden, Dr. Joseph Sugarman and Dr. Randy Schnittman, whose support and confidence are forever appreciated.

The singers and musicians who perform on the recording:

Harold Clausing	Jerry Ray
Wayne Eikenberry	Kathleen Riggs
Evelyn Halus	Kathy Rubbico
Mitch Kaplan	Steve Starkman

ABOUT THE AUTHOR

In the middle of his concert at the famous Forum in Los Angeles, superstar Stevie Wonder stopped the show to acknowledge, in front of thousands of fans, a man who has had much to do with the success and longevity of his vocal career. He wasn't referring to his manager or record producer. He was referring to Seth Riggs—his voice teacher.

And, this isn't just an isolated case. Grateful stars often give credit to this man whose unconventional methods allow them to use the main vehicle for their talent—their voice—to its maximum degree of efficiency and effectiveness.

Whether he has to go on location to a movie set, a concert date, or a recording studio to help a Natalie Cole, a Jeremy Irons, or a Michael Jackson, Seth Riggs has helped many a star—and nervous producer—out of a jam. Recently he gave Waylon Jennings a voice lesson by telephone. The country singer was in Tahoe to open a show with his wife Jessie Colter and his voice was ailing. It was Jennings' first contact with Riggs. However, Riggs was able to get the singer's voice in shape quickly with just a few special exercises.

Seth Riggs's vocal technique and the methods he uses to teach the technique were forged and tempered by the fierce demands placed on the world's top performers, who must often perform several shows a night—night after night! A great deal of money is always at stake, so his clients' voices must be able to function easily, without strain. It is no wonder that whenever singers come to Los Angeles from other parts of the world, producers, directors and fellow performers send them to see his master vocal technician.

Seth began his career at the age of nine as a boy-soprano singing music of Bach and Handel at the Washington National Cathedral in Washington, D.C. His later training, however, reached into all areas of the performing arts. He studied acting with Lee Strasberg, Sandy Meisner, Bobby Lewis, and Frank Silvera; dancing with Peter Gennaro, Matt Mattox, and Luigi. He studied voice with John Charles Thomas, Robert Weede, Tito Schipa, and Keith Davis, and did repertoire coaching with Pierre Bernac, Martial Singher, Leo Taubman, Charles Wadsworth, John Brownlee, Hans Heintz, and Louis Graveure. He joined his first professional union, Actor's Equity, two years before completing his undergraduate degree. After that, he became a member of all the performing unions: AFTRA, SAG, AGVA, AGMA, as well as ACRA (the Association of Canadian Radio Artists).

He spent ten years in New York City. For three years he performed on Broadway, and for six seasons he was a guest artist with the New York City Opera. Yet, in the midst of pursuing his own singing career, he discovered that his greatest talent lay in his ability to help others. After taking a few

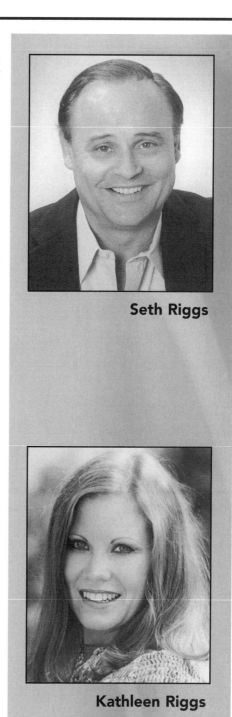

Seth Riggs

Kathleen Riggs

Wendy Warschaw

Associate Vocal Instructor
Los Angeles

Greg Enriquez

Actor, Singer, Lecturer
Las Vegas

lessons with him, singers were able to use their voices more efficiently and consistently than they could using any conventional approach. This encouraged him to take teaching more seriously.

Early in his new career, Seth's success with his students became so well known that many singers left their teachers to study with him. He tried to convince other teachers of the merits of his teaching method, but without success. Nonconventional methods, no matter how well they worked, were frowned on by the teaching establishment. He was kicked out of the National Association of Teachers of Singing and lost positions at the colleges where he taught. Rejected by the establishment, Riggs headed west to Los Angeles, where he has established the most versatile school of vocal technique of our time.

With $330 in his pocket, and a rented truck carrying his motorcycle and music scores, he arrived in L.A. His first show business client was Ann-Margret (sent to him by Allan Carr), who had been "belting" too hard while singing and dancing in Las Vegas. Next, Bob Fosse and Gwen Verdon hired him to prepare Shirley MacLaine's voice for the movie *Sweet Charity*. He was also retained in New York by Richard Rogers, Alan Jay Lerner, Jules Styne, David Merrick and Hal Prince to teach their principal singers. And, as his reputation for getting results grew, so did his list of star clientele. Gregory Peck once asked Frank Sinatra to recommend a good voice teacher for his son Anthony—Sinatra sent him to see Seth Riggs. Mr. Sinatra also suggested to Roger Moore that he send his son Geoffrey to study with Seth. Mr. Riggs is considered the entertainment world's top voice teacher.

But, although Seth Riggs is best known for the stage, screen, recording, and television personalities he works with, his other students have won over a half of a million dollars in prizes, grants, scholarships, and fellowships over the last ten years. These awards include four National Metropolitan Opera Winners, Chicago's WGN, Rockefeller Foundation Grants, the Frank Sinatra Awards, Young Musicians Foundation Awards, Salzburg Mozart Festival Award, National Opera Award, and Fulbright and Rotary Scholarships to Europe. Seth's opera pupils have successful careers singing in Munich, Hamburg, Frankfurt, Saltzberg, Vienna Staatsoper, La Scala, Covent Garden and other major opera houses throughout Europe.

In the summer of 1982, Mr. Riggs replaced two international voice technique teachers at the Banff Centre near Lake Louise in Canada, where he was in charge of vocal technique for 33 opera singers for the Canadian Government. He was also asked to work with 20 young actors from Stratford. His diversity of students—singers of pop, opera, and musical theater, as well as actors and dancers—constantly reaffirms the universality and practicality of his technique.

He draws over 1000 new voice students per year without advertising. Of these, 40 percent are opera, and 60 percent a mixture of musical theatre and pop students. He teaches from his private studio, which converts to a 75-seat recital hall with a 20-foot stage.

He lectures and conducts Master Classes on vocal technique at colleges and universities throughout the United States and Canada. He also has assisted some of the country's foremost doctors who specialize in organic and functional disorders of the voice in vocal therapy (the elimination of vocal nodules, polyps, and various conditions of fibrosis).

Consider a man who believes his best credits include being kicked out of a national singing association and several college music faculties for encouraging pop and musical theatre teaching on an equal footing with opera, and you have Seth Riggs. In the pragmatic world of show business, where time is money, Seth Riggs, whose students have won 96 Grammy awards, is the man professionals turn to for results.

David Stroud

Actor, Singer, Lecturer
San Francisco

John Fluker

Gospel Style Instructor
Los Angeles

INTRODUCTION

What do Michael Jackson and Bernadette Peters have in common? They, and many other music professionals and celebrities in the entertainment field, have endorsed the author's method of vocal training as a key to their vocal success. Here, these celebrities tell how this method helped them use their voices most effectively and survive the vocal stresses of live performances and long recording sessions.

A great many voice teachers, in their effort to teach a workable vocal technique, take away a singer's style and the individuality that established his career in the first place. A great teacher is able to direct a singer toward a healthier, more extensive use of his voice without losing that special quality that sets him apart. Seth Riggs is such a teacher. His assistance on my albums ET, Thriller, Bad, Dangerous and HIStory and his traveling with me on the 1988 World Tour, continues to confirm my confidence in this approach.

Michael Jackson

*Producer, Recording Artist, Singer
Los Angeles*

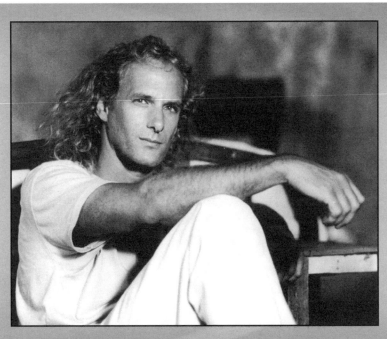

Not long ago, I had the honor of performing with Luciano Pavarotti at a benefit concert in his home town of Modena, Italy. It was, of course, a most inspiring event and caused me to fall eternally in love with opera.

When I returned to the United States, I contacted my great friend and mentor, Seth Riggs, who introduced me to the incredible "bel canto" usage of the voice that I had first heard Pavarotti use in Modena.

Expanding my voice and taking it to new operatic levels has meant a lot of diligent study, but the result has been phenomenally rewarding. My fans embrace my performances of the arias I have added to my concerts, and I am currently in the process of recording an entire album of classic tenor arias.

Seth's instruction has been invaluable to me—the extended ease and ranges of my voice, and the quality of my opera singing have vastly improved. I am deeply grateful to him and his New York opera associate, William Schuman, for all they continue to do to help take my voice to the next level.

Michael Bolton

Singer, Composer
New York City

I want to thank Seth for helping me build a strong "connection" into the gospel sound and ranges. (No strain and no pain, honey.) We're "moving" with a new vocal, mental, and physical health. Thank you for all those warm-ups for my Unforgettable album.

Natalie Cole

Singer
Los Angeles

*E*ight shows a week with a Broadway show, or fourteen shows a week in Las Vegas or Atlantic City—you have to be secure vocally to survive.

Seth has helped me establish a solid foundation of vocal technique, so I can meet any vocal challenge squarely and with confidence. Singers are always being directed musically by someone. It's great to have a knowledgeable vocal point of view to protect your performance and your vocal health.

Bernadette Peters

Actress, Singer
New York City

*M*y work with Seth enabled me to reach a new level of performance. He helped me to meld three disparate voices into one fluid instrument with greater range, one that I can count on eight times a week, even in the most demanding situations.

Douglas Sills

Actor, Singer (male lead in The Scarlet Pimpernel)
New York City

*W*hen I played the lead role in Miss Saigon ("Kim"), I only had to sing up to E 1½ octaves above middle C. Now that I am studying with Seth Riggs, I can go much higher and with a lot of confidence. Expanding my range helps me sing R&B. Seth helped me gain a lot of self-confidence in my singing—now I am brave. Confidence through proper vocal technique is the most important thing a teacher can teach a student.

Leila Florentino

Actress, Singer
Los Angeles

After 35 years or so, singing night after night, the "wear and tear" on your voice can become extreme. Balancing the "bridge area" from the lower pitches (chest) to your "head voice" is critical. "Pulling up" the bottom pitches or "belting" can cause a "wobble" so severe that your singing career can be shortened drastically. This technique of "balancing" the break areas, so that there is no "audible change" as you "pass through" from "bottom to top" is invaluable. It is your first line of defense against vocal deterioration.

Nancy Dussault

*Actress, Singer, Lecturer
New York, Los Angeles*

When I first came to Hollywood, I came into contact with Seth. I had studied in New York City with a principal tenor at the Metropolitan Opera. I had trouble with my "top." Constantly taping the exercises and applying the "bridging balance" freed my voice to a point where I could sing both baritone and tenor ranges through high C. This technique has become an intimate, personal confident knowledge of how to keep myself in a decent, healthy vocal condition during those rigorous Broadway schedules.

Peter Gallagher

*Actor, Singer
New York*

For 2½ years I had the great opportunity to play the lead role in Evita at the Alvin Theater on Broadway. Evita is one of the most demanding vocal roles in modern musical theater. There is no spoken dialogue but there are 2½ hours of hard singing, including a high "belted middle," which rides high into the "black gospel" sound. It is exciting, but you could annihilate your voice unless you know what you're doing. Seth Riggs gave me the technique and personal ability to guide myself vocally and guard against vocal abuse and fatigue.

Derin Altay

*Actress, Singer
New York City*

*T*he technique that Seth Riggs gives his students is extraordinary in an art form riddled with guessing and false understanding of the way the vocal chords work. He teaches how to get through the bridge of the voice—easily and confidently.

Clifford David

Actor, Singer, Lecturer
Los Angeles

I've been a "belter" all of my life. I didn't even think I had a head voice. When Seth connected my middle voice, I was able to drop the wear of 20 years of hard singing.

Carol Burnett

Actress, Singer
Hawaii

*A*t this time of my life I'm finally getting my voice together. I had always thought that singing high C's and above was like lifting weights, and that I just wasn't strong enough or just didn't have the gift. Thank God, neither reason was the case.

Seth taught me that the top of my range (among other things) was dependent on the release of my middle voice. That way I didn't have to break into falsetto above a certain point. Now I can sing to the high C and E-flat above, in an even line without strain.

When I sang the lead role in Phantom of the Opera, *this technique really came through for me. The Phantom, besides the heavy, emotional speaking demands, covers two octaves of singing range. Thank you Seth. I wish I had met you sooner.*

Robert Guillaume

Actor
Los Angeles

*A*s a composer, you usually have an idea of how you'd like your music sung. I like the singer to communicate the text with as beautiful a vocal sound as possible. However, if vocal problems get in the way, the effectiveness can be destroyed on many levels. I've always enjoyed Seth Riggs's singers, because they sing evenly in many keys with power and control. Thus, I have the freedom to find the best "presence" for the text, the voice and the chart.

Marvin Hamlisch

Composer, Pianist
New York City

*S*ome years ago we needed a voice coach to assist Shirley MacLaine to get her vocal chops in shape for the film Sweet Charity. Bob Fosse and Gwen Verdon recommended Seth Riggs for the project. When I arrived in Los Angeles to set the vocal keys for Shirley, I decided that she was able to use whichever key suited the action of the character in the scene. That meant she could sing in several different keys. I always appreciated the quality work that Shirley and Seth put in to properly prepare her voice for the role of Charity.

Cy Coleman

Composer, Pianist
New York City

*S*eth and I have been together going on a quarter century. Seth vocalizes me from basso profundo B♭ to tenor high B♭. This sounds like a wild range (three octaves), but I perform in 1½–2 octaves at the most. It is free, connected and has a steady vibrato. When I think of some of the extravagances I've put my body through, I'm lucky to still be able to sing decently.

Paul Williams

Composer, Performer
Los Angeles

When the "tracks" are hot, sweetening and balance still to consider, and release dates pending, there is precious little time to accommodate an artist's vocal indisposition. It has been my experience that myriad problems such as vocal fatigue, lack of control and diminishing vocal quality can be overcome or eliminated by a solid, practical vocal technique. Seth Riggs has an uncanny ability to prepare vocalists so that there is little time lost to the usual vocal problems. His assistance during the Michael Jackson 1988 World Tour kept Michael tuned up like a Ferrari.

Quincy Jones

Producer, Arranger
Los Angeles

A couple of years ago, Stevie Wonder put me on a counsel phone hook-up with Seth and we arranged to start some voice study. Soon I became involved in Seth's technique. I bought the book and also sat in on lessons with a junior "Star Search" winner who got a contract with CBS Records (whom I was producing). Seth's vocal approach makes the high notes solid and easy, with no need to resort to falsetto (unless for some special effect). This approach is a valuable addition to making your styling easy, always available and extending the life of your voice.

Luther Vandross

Producer, Singer
Los Angeles

I first met Seth Riggs after corrective surgery. My bad vocal habits had caught up with me, and I was forced to find a more correct way to sing. That was in 1967. Today I still experiment with many different vocal styles and qualities, and the muscular freedom to do that is the result of my work with Seth. I slip occasionally, but Seth is always there to rebalance my voice. Seth has been my only voice teacher.

Stevie Wonder

Recording Artist, Singer
Los Angeles

Unlike the stars whose endorsements appear at the front of this book, you may not be able to arrange for a personal lesson with the author. But this book and accompanying CDs can be the next best thing to it. Here are some guidelines and suggestions to help you get the most out of this training program.

1. Is this book meant only for those studying a certain kind of music, such as classical music or popular music?

No. This book teaches a vocal technique based on speech-level singing. Speech-level singing is a way of using your voice that allows you to sing freely and clearly anywhere in your range, with all your words clearly understood. Since you are not learning what to sing but rather how to sing, you can apply this technique to any type of music.

2. Can anyone learn this technique, or do you need prior singing experience or musical training?

This book has been designed to be used by singers at any level—from beginner to advanced.

3. Can I study this book without a teacher?

Yes. You can study either with or without a teacher. You can probably progress more easily and faster if you can find a teacher familiar with this method of teaching to guide you. Otherwise, you should be able to study successfully on your own by following the instructions in this book and on the accompanying CDs. But you should pay special attention to the precautions advised.

4. What are the precautions advised in learning this technique?

As valuable as the exercises in this book are for training your voice, any exercise can be overworked or misused to where it will do you more harm than good. You don't develop your

Singing jazz means a great many syncopated rhythms and a wide range of pitches. Over the years I'd picked up some bad vocal habits which began to cause vocal strain and fatigue. In other words, I'd begun to "trash" my voice. By helping me take pressure off my chest range and getting into my head coordination, Seth Riggs contributed a relaxation and, ultimately, a better longevity for my career.

Al Jarreau

Recording Artist, Singer
Los Angeles

voice by pushing it to its limit. You develop it by gradually conditioning it to work efficiently with a balanced coordination.

When doing the exercises, please follow along with the material in the book and the accompanying CDs as my students and I demonstrate how each of the exercises should be done. It is important that you do each exercise *correctly* before you proceed to the next.

5. Do I need to study the "Basic Principles" before starting the practical exercises?

That's really up to you. If you are working with a teacher, you should follow your teacher's recommendations. However, if you are working on your own, the "Basic Principles" section will help you better understand how your voice works and how this method of voice training works. You will then be able to progress more quickly.

Don't worry about memorizing every detail. When you feel you understand the material, go on to the exercises. As you do the exercises, if you find an instruction unclear or have difficulty carrying it out, go back and study more closely the text or illustration that applies. A glossary has been provided at the end of the book to make it easier to locate definitions of unfamiliar words.

6. Are there any guidelines for doing the practical exercises?

These are supplied on the CDs and in the accompanying text. If you have personal questions about your training or career, or how to take the best care of your voice, you may find some answers in the two sections at the end of the book—"The Author Speaks Out" and "Health and Care of the Singer's Voice."

I'd never sung before, my voice is as low as a bass and I'd never tried "higher ranges." I began a film where the script called on my character to sing. I figured they would probably dub my voice. The studio sent me to Seth. Not only did I wind up singing my own songs, but we almost did a song from Leonard Bernstein's Mass. I know now how to get from my deep range into the high with no change in quality. In short, I'm not nervous about singing anymore.

Whoopi Goldberg

Comedian, Actress
Los Angeles

How Your Voice Works

The Creation of Vocal Tone

There are two factors involved in making vocal tone—*vocal cord vibration* and *resonance*.

1. Vocal cord vibration

The air you exhale from your lungs works with your vocal cords to create an initial tone.

2. Resonance

That tone is then modified and amplified as it travels through the spaces above your vocal cords before leaving your mouth.

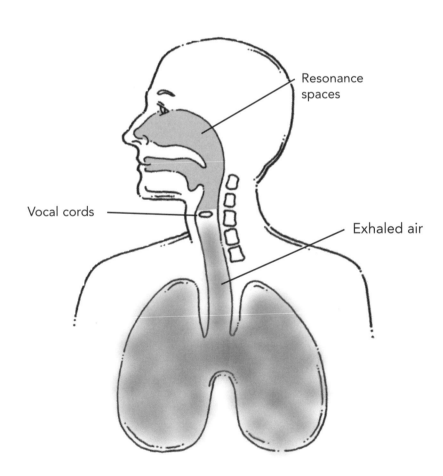

Let's examine these factors more closely.

*T*rying to coordinate rehearsal schedules between the end of one project and the beginning of another can be hectic. There never seems to be enough time to prepare as well as you would like.

One morning in 1967, Allan Carr called to tell me he had found a vocal technique teacher who taught a technique that was efficient and quickly learned. The teacher was Seth Riggs. The technique has served me well, has kept me together vocally through many difficult and trying situations.

Ann-Margret

Actress, Singer
Los Angeles

Vocal Cord Vibration—Where Your Voice Begins

Located at the top of your windpipe (*trachea*—pronounced tray-key-uh) is a group of cartilages, ligaments, and muscles that function as a single unit. This unit, known commonly as your voicebox, is your *larynx* (pronounced lä [as in cat] -rinks). Inside your larynx, attached from front to back, are the main muscles of your larynx—your vocal cords.

The location of your vocal cords

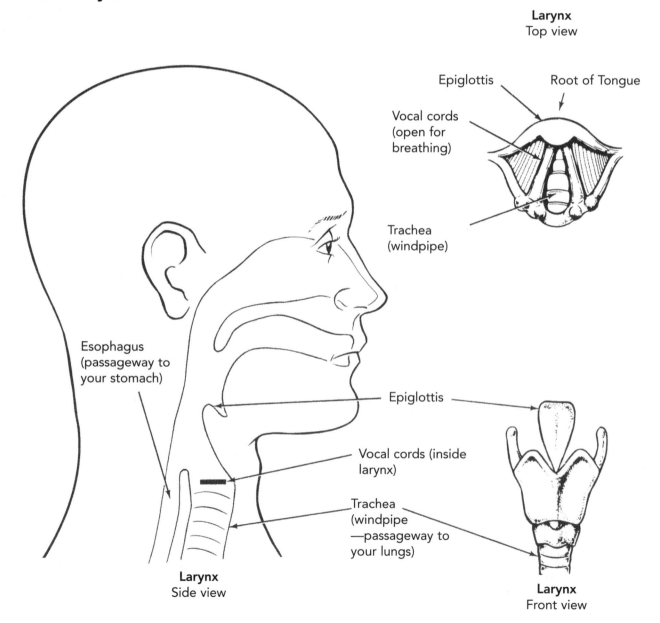

Larynx
Top view

Epiglottis

Root of Tongue

Vocal cords
(open for
breathing)

Trachea
(windpipe)

Esophagus
(passageway to
your stomach)

Epiglottis

Vocal cords (inside
larynx)

Trachea
(windpipe
—passageway to
your lungs)

Larynx
Side view

Larynx
Front view

If your vocal cords are closed (or almost closed) at the same time you exhale, air pressure builds up below them.

Vocal cords closed
Front view

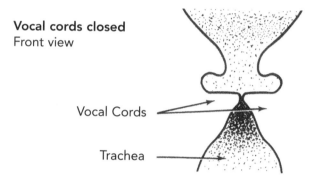

Vocal Cords

Trachea

When the air pressure becomes too great for your vocal cords to hold back, the cords are blown apart. The sudden release of air pushes the air molecules above your cords together and *outward*, creating a wave of compressed air molecules—a *sound* wave.

Vocal cords open

Wave of compressed air

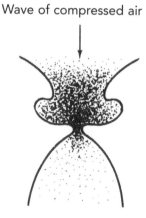

Once the air pressure is released, your vocal cords spring back to their closed (or almost closed) position.

Vocal cords closed

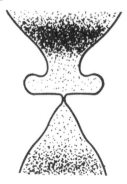

I used to sing when I was a kid. I think I was a tenor. I even flirted with the idea of singing for a living, but I could never find anyone to help me get into my high voice properly.

Acting took over and, lo and behold, I got into a part where I had to sing. The producers called in Seth, and, first lesson, I was well into my head voice and began to learn how to make the "transition," through the "passaggio," from my chest into the head voice. It is still developing, but I know "where I'm going" when I sing.

Armand Assante
Actor
Los Angeles

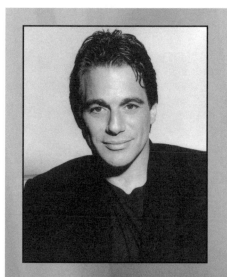

I love to entertain, therefore I have to study dancing and singing. Since I began to work with Seth, I have a steady, even vibrato much higher than I ever thought I could sing. Would you believe it? I'm a tenor!

Tony Danza

Actor, Singer, Dancer
Los Angeles

As your vocal cords come back together again and again, they are blown apart again and again—creating a *series of sound waves,* which is picked up by the listener's ear. This process is called *vibration.*

**Vocal cord vibration
creates sound waves**

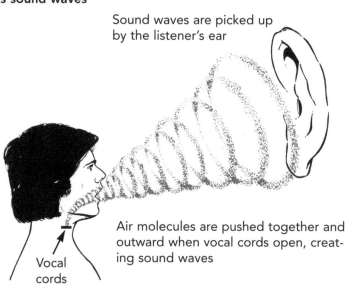

Sound waves are picked up by the listener's ear

Air molecules are pushed together and outward when vocal cords open, creating sound waves

Vocal cords

But, now let's examine vocal cord vibration as it relates to the more demanding requirements of the singer's voice. To do this, we must consider *breath support* and *vocal cord adjustment.*

Breath support

Normally, your respiratory system—which you use to send air to your vocal cords—operates *automatically,* without any conscious effort. Its primary function is to supply your body with the life substance, oxygen, and eliminate the waste product, carbon dioxide.

Inhalation begins when too much carbon dioxide builds up inside your body.

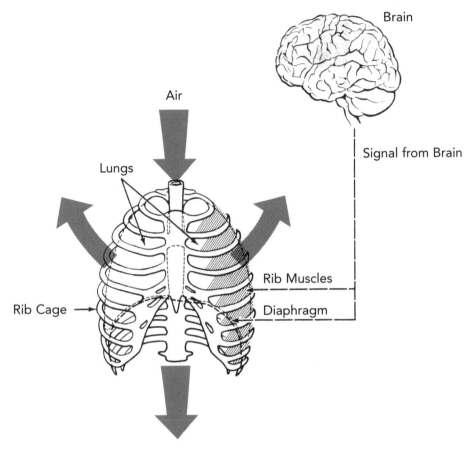

Normal Inhalation

1. **Signal**
   Your brain signals your breathing muscles that your body needs oxygen.

2. **Action**
   Your diaphragm—your main breathing muscle—descends (flattens), enlarging your chest cavity at the bottom, while your rib muscles lift your rib cage, enlarging your chest cavity at the sides. This creates a vacuum inside your chest cavity.

3. **Result**
   Air fills your lungs, as the outside air rushes in to fill the vacuum.

   Exhalation begins as soon as inhalation has taken place.

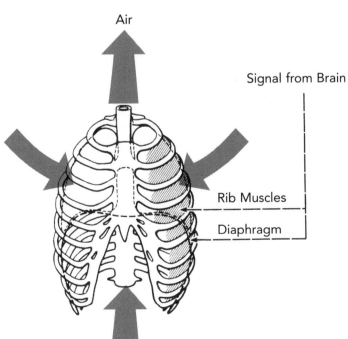

Normal Exhalation

1. **Signal**
   Your brain signals your breathing muscles that your body needs to get rid of carbon dioxide.

2. **Action**
   Your diaphragm and rib muscles relax. The diaphragm returns to its up position and your rib cage comes down. This allows your lungs to shrink back.

3. **Result**
   Air is squeezed out of your lungs.

   In singing and speaking, however, you can regulate inhalation, as long as it doesn't interfere with your body's requirements for life support.

Inhalation During Singing

1. **Signal**
   Your brain signals your breathing muscles that you need a supply of air to make sound.

2. **Action**
   Same as normal inhalation, except you regulate how much air you need and at what rate you will take it in. Be sure your chest remains "comfortably high" (see p. 86) and that your abdominal (stomach) muscles are relaxed to let your diaphragm descend easily, without any resistance.

3. **Result**
   Air fills your lungs.

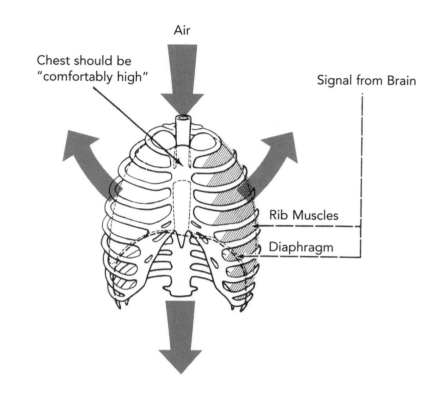

Air

Chest should be "comfortably high"

Signal from Brain

Rib Muscles

Diaphragm

Exhalation During Singing

1. **Singing**
   Your brain signals your breathing muscles that you need to send air to your vocal cords.

2. **Action**
   Not the same as normal exhalation. To be able to regulate the amount of air you send to your vocal cords, you must be able to control your rate of exhalation. Your rib muscles, therefore, continue to keep your rib cage (thus your lungs) expanded, while your abdominal muscles take over control. Your abdominal muscles push your diaphragm (in a state of flexible tension) up steadily and slowly against your lungs.

3. **Result**
   Air is released to your vocal cords as needed.

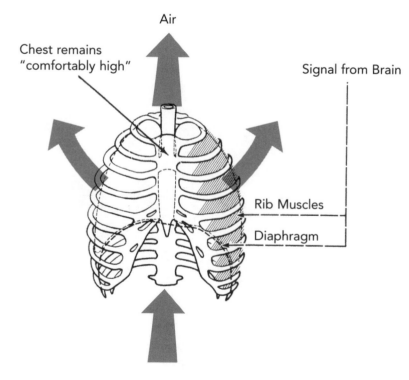

Air

Chest remains "comfortably high"

Signal from Brain

Rib Muscles

Diaphragm

Breathing for singing is a very relaxed process. When we say you can regulate it, we only mean *you allow it to happen* so that inhalation and exhalation are done in a way that best suits your musical needs. You do not have to *work* at breathing correctly, unless you have poor posture or a tendency to raise your chest and shoulders and take shallow breaths. Nor do you need to do any special exercises to strengthen your breathing muscles. Your diaphragm (pronounced dïe-uh-fram), rib muscles, and abdominal muscles are already strong enough for your needs as a singer.

If you maintain good posture when you sing, and are careful not to let your chest "collapse" as you exhale, your diaphragm is able to move freely and be regulated by your abdominal muscles *automatically*. There is no need to consciously exert tension in those muscles. If you try to directly control your breathing muscles when you sing, the extra tension in your body will only cause your vocal cords to overtense—to jam up.

Very little air is required to produce a good tone. Even for a loud tone, the amount of air you use need only be enough to *support* the vibration of your vocal cords—no more, no less—so that your tone is produced without any effort or strain. Just as trying to control your breathing muscles directly will cause your vocal cords to jam up, so will using too much air. That's because, when you sing, your cords are instinctively committed to holding back (or at least trying to hold back) any amount of air you send their way. And, the more air you send them, the tighter your cords have to get to hold it back.

You know you have proper breath support when there is a *balance* between air and muscle. There will be a mutual and simultaneous coordination of the proper amount of air with the proper adjustment of your vocal cords.

Vocal cord adjustment

As your exhaled air reaches your vocal cords, your vocal cords, assisted by the other muscles of your larynx, adjust with your breath flow to create the *pitch* and *intensity* of your tone. When we talk about the action of your vocal cords, we are actually talking about the combined efforts of all the muscles in your larynx that influence their activity.

Balance equals support

Imbalance equals effort and strain

The Muscles of your Larynx

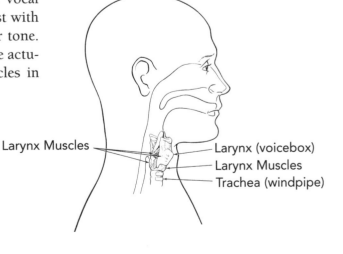

Larynx Muscles

Larynx (voicebox)
Larynx Muscles
Trachea (windpipe)

Pitch (frequency of vibration)

Definition

Pitch is the *frequency* of completed vibration cycles in a given tone. It is measured in *hertz* (cycles per second). The human ear has a range of 20 to 20,000 hertz.

How pitch applies to your voice

Pitch is determined by how often, or how *frequently,* your vocal cords vibrate (open and close), which is determined by the tension in your cords. The more tension there is in your vocal cords, the more quickly they will return to their closed position once they are blown apart. The greater the frequency of vibration, the higher the pitch.

When we talk about vocal cord tension, however, we don't mean the type of tension that results in vocal cord strain. They are two different things. Vocal cord tension, which *you shouldn't feel* if you are singing correctly, is created by the interaction of the muscles within your larynx as they help your vocal cords balance against the air pressure from your lungs. The kind of tension that can lead to vocal cord strain, on the other hand, is created when you use the muscles *outside* your larynx to pull on and tighten around your larynx to control the pitch and intensity of your tone.

Intensity (force of vibration)

Definition

Intensity is the *force* of each sound wave on the ear. It is measured in units of loudness called *decibels.* The relative degrees of loudness are called *dynamics.*

How intensity applies to your voice

Intensity is determined by the *force* of the air released by your vocal cords, which is determined by how long your vocal cords can hold back the mounting air pressure before they finally blow open. The louder the tone, the more air pressure and vocal cord resistance is needed to produce that tone.

In softer tones, your vocal cords (offering less resistance) open sooner and stay open longer in each vibration. In louder tones, your vocal cords (offering more resistance) take longer to blow open but then close again almost immediately.

You don't necessarily need more air when you sing loudly than when you sing softly—just more air *pressure.* Because your vocal cords stay closed longer in louder tones, little air escapes unused. Air pressure, therefore, has a chance to build up to the point where, when it finally does blow your vocal cords open, the *force* of the air released (and thus the soundwave) is much greater.

Pitch also affects loudness because the ear is more sensitive to higher frequencies.

Although your vocal cords continually adjust to meet the pitch and dynamic (the degree of intensity or loudness) requirements for each note you sing, we simply refer to all vocal cord adjustments in terms of the physical sensations they produce in the singer. Your chest *voice*, or *chest register*, refers to the lowest tones in your range, while your *head voice*, or *head register*, refers to the highest ones. The part of your range where qualities of both head and chest overlap is called your *middle voice*, or *middle register*. Yet, the sensations you *feel* are the result of proper vocal cord function, and the resultant balance in that "bridging" coordination.

Resonance—Why Your Voice Is Unique

Between the time your tone leaves your vocal cords and the time it exits your mouth, it goes through a process of transformation. The interconnected spaces above your larynx—including the surface condition of the walls which define those spaces—reinforce and augment sound waves of certain frequencies, while damping or even eliminating others. This process is called *resonance*.

Your resonance system

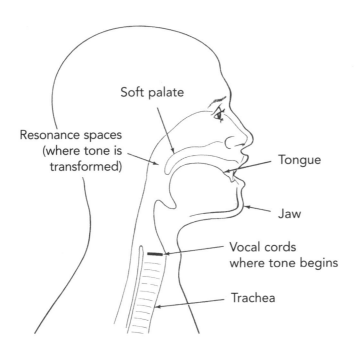

Soft palate

Resonance spaces (where tone is transformed)

Tongue

Jaw

Vocal cords where tone begins

Trachea

I first began to study singing when I was 11 years old. Besides connecting my "chest" and "head," Seth tricked me into an extremely high area, which, as we continued to work, began to join into the rest of my vocal range. I signed with my first major label at age 11. From that early age, I always vocalized and performed over 3 ½ octaves. These days, when singers have begun to use stratospheric high notes, I've never had to fear extremely low to extremely high notes. Thank you, Seth.

Shanice Wilson

Singer
Los Angeles

Physical sensations

A by-product of resonance activity, as we have already mentioned, is the creation of physical sensations in the singer. Low tones feel like they are in your throat and mouth and, at times, can even be felt in your chest—thus the term *chest voice*. As you sing higher, your voice (if you are singing correctly) feels like it leaves your throat and mouth and goes more and more behind your soft palate until, finally, it feels like it goes out the back of your head—thus the term *head voice*.

But the physical sensations you experience have nothing to do with what the listener actually hears. What these sensations *can* do, however, is help guide you in the correct and consistent use of your voice. There will be more about this in the training program itself.

Vocal cord vibration determines the *initial quality* of your tone, but resonance determines the *final quality*—the quality that makes your voice sound different from anyone else's. That difference is due mainly to the unique size and shape of your own resonance system.

Both vocal cord vibration and resonance should work independently. Yet, problems with one always affect the ability of the other to do its job. Fortunately, these problems can be avoided with good singing technique.

Middle Voice
A blend of chest and head sensations. It's the middle.

Head Voice
Highest tones feel like they travel out of the back of your head

Chest Voice
Lowest tones feel like they travel out of your mouth

What to Remember

The two factors involved in creating vocal tone are:

1. *Vocal cord vibration.* The air you exhale from your lungs works with your vocal cords to create the *pitch* and *intensity* of your initial tone. Breathing for singing is a very relaxed process in which very little air is required to produce a good tone

2. *Resonance.* The initial tone is *modified* and *amplified* as it travels through the spaces above your vocal cords before leaving your mouth. Each person has a different resonance system that makes his or her own voice unique. Physical sensations, which are a by-product of resonance activity, can help guide you in the correct and consistent use of your voice .

How Your Voice Works Best

The Natural Technique of Speech-Level Singing

Most singers use excessive muscular effort when they sing. Muscles the body normally uses to chew and swallow food, as well as open the throat wider when it needs to get oxygen into the lungs quickly, are used to manipulate the larynx—forcing it up or down. This is done to accomplish a difficult pitch, increase intensity, or "improve" the quality of one's tone. We call these muscles the *outer muscles,* because they are located outside the larynx.

Whenever you use your outer muscles to control your voice in any way, however, you prevent the free vibration of your vocal cords inside your larynx, and alter the relationship (and the overall condition) of the resonance spaces above your larynx. The result is a labored and unbalanced sound.

Only when your larynx is in a relaxed, stable position can your vocal cords adjust easily with your breath flow, to create the pitch and intensity of your initial tone. And, only when your larynx is in a relaxed, stable position will your final tone contain a balance of top, middle, and bottom harmonic qualities—like a good stereo system—so you never sound "muddy" on low notes or "splatty" on high ones.

Yet, there's another important reason why your larynx must be kept free of outer-muscle interference. Many of these muscles are involved in the production of speech sounds, and their interference in the tone-making process inevitably disrupts the word-making process as well. It's hard to form vowels and make consonants when the muscles controlling the movement of your tongue and jaw, for instance, are also trying to control your tone. Hence, voice production using the muscles outside your larynx is a hopeless battle in which both your tone *and* your words become the casualties.

Right:
Speech level

Wrong:
Reaching for high notes

Your Speech Level—a Foundation for Vocal Freedom

Generally, when you speak in a quiet, comfortable manner, your outer muscles do not interfere with the functioning of your larynx. That's because tone is not your primary concern—communication is. Therefore, your larynx is allowed to rest in a relatively stable, or what we call a *speech-level,* position. This is the ideal vocal condition or *posture* with which to sing.

If you can learn to initiate and maintain your tone with this comfortable *speech-level posture* when you sing, you can sing with the same easily produced voice you use—or should be using—when you speak. Nothing will feel any different in your throat or mouth. Both your tone and words will feel natural and sound natural.

But be careful Speech-level singing doesn't mean "sing like you speak!"

Wrong:
Reaching for low notes

*W*hen I write a song, I need a vocal range and control that allows me complete freedom to express my feelings. Seth works my voice over three octaves.

So far, there have been no vocal limitations for me in my work. With this particular approach to singing, I can adapt my voice to sing God's praises in a Gospel style, sing a romantic ballad or up-tune, even high ranging coloratura (G and A and above high C) for my own backup overlap.

Deniece Williams

Composer, Singer
Los Angeles

Singing High Tones

RIGHT: Speech-level production

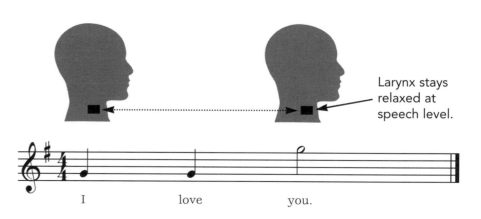

Larynx stays relaxed at speech level.

I   love   you.

Result: Tone is "bright" and "full."
Words sound clear and are easy to produce

WRONG: Larynx forced up.

Larynx is forced up. Swallowing muscles may also be squeezing around your throat and larynx.

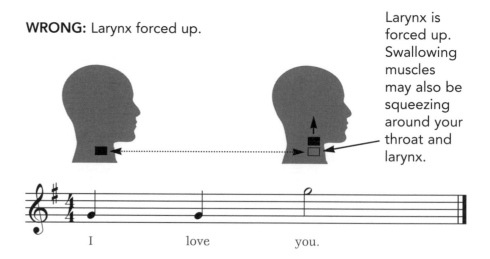

I   love   you.

Result: Tone is "strident" and "brittle."
Words sound distorted and are difficult to produce.

Singing Low Tones

RIGHT: Speech-level production

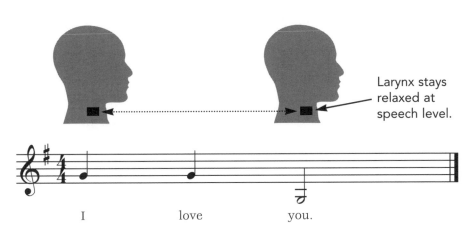

Larynx stays relaxed at speech level.

I   love   you.

Result: Tone is "bright" and "full."
Words sound clear and are easy to produce

WRONG: Larynx forced down.

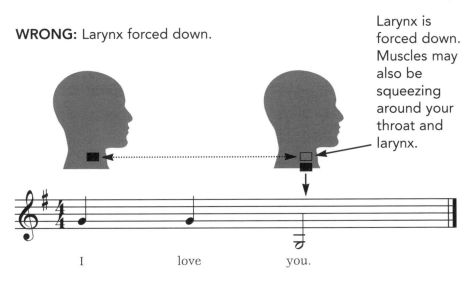

Larynx is forced down. Muscles may also be squeezing around your throat and larynx.

I   love   you.

Result: Tone is "dark" and "throaty."
Words sound distorted and are difficult to produce.

When he believes in your vocal ability, he is relentless in making sure you never back away from your full potential—instilling confidence is the true gift of a great teacher. Because of Seth Riggs, I'm meeting any vocal challenge I've ever wanted to—I'm relaxed and having so much fun.

Kim Basinger

Actress
Los Angeles

When you talk, you only use a limited pitch and dynamic range of tones, so it doesn't require a great deal of cord tension to create those tones. In order to meet your needs for the higher pitch and greater dynamic levels often required in singing, however, your vocal cords must be able to achieve greater degrees of tension. Increased cord tension is what brings your cords back together more quickly each time they are blown apart, when you need to sing a higher tone. Increased cord tension is what enables your cords to hold back that extra bit of air pressure before they finally blow open, when you need to sing a louder tone.

If your vocal cords and the other muscles in your larynx are unable to provide the required tension themselves, you can be sure that your outer muscles will volunteer their help. But, that's the kind of help you don't want! *Any* outer muscle participation in the vibration process will only cause you vocal problems by pulling you off your speech level.

Speech-Level Singing—Feeling and Sounding Natural

You should be able to sing through your entire range—from the lowest notes of your chest voice, up through the highest notes of your head voice—in a smooth, even, or what we call *connected* manner, and still maintain a relaxed speech-level posture.

Singing low notes

The lower part of your range is never a problem as long as you are careful not to press down with your larynx in an effort to scrape the bottom of your range to get your lowest notes, or do anything in your throat or mouth that alters your speech-level posture. An example of the latter would be "creating more space" in your throat or mouth, to achieve a "deep, rich, resonant" quality.

To begin with, the lowest note in your range should be the *lowest note you can sing easily* while still maintaining your speech-level posture. As far as the resonance quality of your voice, it should be whatever results naturally from that same speech-level posture. You should never try to *make* your voice resonant. You should never try to *make* it do anything.

Singing high notes

It doesn't take a genius to know that a singer's biggest problem, at least from a vocal standpoint, is singing high notes. Therefore, we will be most concerned about extending your range upward. As you free your upper range, your lower range will also increase because, when your outer muscles are relaxed in the vibration process, they allow your larynx, thus your vocal cords, to relax as well.

Some time ago, MCA Records suggested I work with Seth Riggs in order to get my "gospel chops" in shape. In the middle of our work, along comes the role of Charity in Sweet Charity for the Los Angeles and New York revivals. Charity was a "belter," but now I can't wait to "get down" with that "high gospel" sound and style. Seth's technique makes it easy.

Debbie Allen

Director, Actress, Singer
Los Angeles

The passage areas of your range

As you sing higher into your range, you quickly encounter areas where muscular and/or resonance activity make it difficult to negotiate smooth transitions between vocal cord adjustments. Most singers know these areas all too well. They are places where the voice jams up, suddenly shifts in quality, or even breaks—things that can discourage someone from ever exploring the full potential of his/her voice.

We, however, refer to these areas as *passage areas*. That's because, when you approach them the right way, they become *passage ways between where you are coming from and where you want to go in your vocal range.*

Singing through the passage areas

Your first passage area is the most critical. It's where your outer muscles (if they haven't done so already) are most likely to enter into the adjustment process. When they do, they pull on and tighten around the outside of your larynx in an effort to stretch your vocal cords to get the necessary tension for the pitch or dynamic level you require. But, as we have said, stretching your cords in this manner causes your *entire* singing mechanism—tone and words—to jam up! Fortunately, there is a better and much easier way to stretch your vocal cords to achieve the necessary tensions without disrupting your tone-making process *or* your word-making process.

The key is to do less in order to do more. To be specific, *the higher you sing, the less air you should use.* When you reduce the amount of air you send to your vocal cords, you make it possible for the muscles *inside* your larynx to stretch your vocal cords by themselves. Your outer muscles are less likely to interfere because there isn't as much air to hold back.* *Your outer muscles will interfere in the vibration process whenever you use more air than your vocal cords and the other muscles inside your larynx are able to handle.*

*You don't need a lot of air to sing loudly (see "Intensity" on page 28).

*S*eth Riggs teaches a technique that doesn't detract from the basic quality of the actors' spoken sound. Actors Studio West is most appreciative of his classes, and lack of intimidation for actors when approaching the act of singing.

Mark Rydell/Martin Landau/Martin Ritt

Actors Studio West
Los Angeles

I have studied with Seth for over a year-and-a-half and I have enjoyed it immensely. My ear, power and vocal production have improved greatly and I believe that Seth's technique is responsible. His method joins the falsetto with the lower voice by strengthening the middle, or bridge, voice. The technique is simple... and it works!

Bette Midler

Recording Artist, Singer
Los Angeles

The Passage Areas: Women

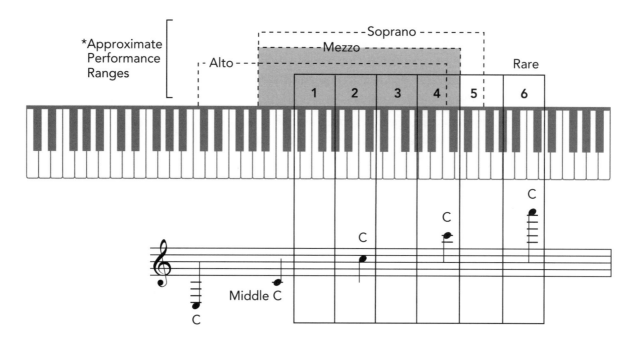

The Passage Areas: Men

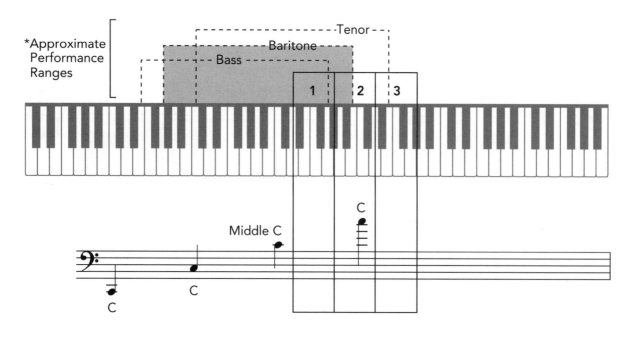

*These are approximate ranges. There are individuals whose ranges extend beyond, but they are exceptions.

Vocal cord thinning

When your vocal cords are stretched, they begin to thin. And the thinner your cords get, the less cord "weight" there is for your exhaled air to move. When the *thinning* takes place at your speech level, however, your cords are able to thin without disrupting your tone or words.

Vocal cord shortening

Then, something very interesting takes place when your vocal cords reach the point where they can't thin (be stretched) any farther—the vibrating *length* of your cords begins to "shorten." Let me explain why and how it happens.

Your vocal cords never open all at once and then close all at once when they vibrate. Even in your lowest tones, your vocal cords open from *front* to *back* and close from *back* to *front*. That's because they are more flexible the closer they get to where they attach to the inside front of your larynx (where your Adam's apple is), and air breaks through that point first.

If you continue to use less and less air past the point where your cords have thinned as far as possible, the back ends of your cords stay together, with less and less of the front part opening and closing. This also means, however, that they open and close much faster, increasing the frequency of vibration which continues to raise the pitch of your tone.

If, like the initial thinning, this *shortening* can take place at your speech level, you can continue to sing easily through the rest of your passage areas with your tone and word production intact. You will be able to extend your range far beyond what most singers can only dream about.

As your vocal cords begin to thin and shorten automatically when you sing, you become less aware of your passage areas. Eventually you come to think of your chest, middle, and head voices as a *single voice*—connected in the way it's produced and connected in quality!

*L*aying down vocal tracks between 12 a.m. one day and 4 a.m. the next can kill your voice. Since beginning vocal study with Seth Riggs, I never lose my ability to sing at nearly any hour. I'm a pianist and when it comes to singing, I've always been extravagant. Now that I've learned about taking high pitches in a connected "head" coordination, I don't have to pull "chest" voice like I have in the past. It's a vocal direction I've needed, because it buys a longer, sustaining health for my voice.

James Ingram
Recording Artist, Singer
Los Angeles

Speech-level singing is a "natural" technique in which your voice is:

1. *Produced without effort.* When you don't allow the muscles outside your larynx—your outer muscles—to interfere with your tone-making process, your vocal cords are able to more easily balance with your breath flow. Also, when you free your tone-making process, you free your word-making process as well, letting you produce all your words easily and clearly.

2. *Balanced in quality.* A relaxed and stable larynx results in a stable resonance system in which your voice always contains an appropriate balance of top, middle, and bottom harmonic qualities, no matter where in your range you sing.

What to Remember

How to Get Your Voice to Work for You

I've been singing since I was a child. Always, the "chest" into the "head" voice was a sticky problem. I now have a firm grasp on the "connection" in my middle. I can lean into a gospel, R&B styling with much more power, knowing that I won't get caught in "pure chest belting"—what a relief.

Marilyn McCoo

Singer
Los Angeles

The Training Process

Training your voice, as you may have guessed, means learning to coordinate and strengthen the muscles in your larynx so you can sing with speech-level posture over a wide pitch and dynamic range. Coordination and strength are most easily developed by doing special exercises. You don't control your voice directly by working on or thinking about breath support, vocal cord adjustments, or resonance. These things are all *by-products* of speech-level singing. They happen *automatically* when you condition your larynx not to move, by relaxing your outer muscles and by allowing your vocal cords to thin and then shorten for higher notes to insure that your outer muscles *stay* relaxed.

As you do the exercises in the training program following this section, you will memorize the physical sensations you experience in your voice as you do each exercise correctly. Everything else will take care of itself.

Developing Coordination—The First Step

Coordination of your voice at your speech level must be developed before you can begin to build strength in your voice. As you do the exercises, don't feel you have to sing them loudly. That's not important. If you try to sing too loudly (using too much air) too soon, your outer muscles will never give up their pulling and tightening reflexes. Have patience.

You must first eliminate any outer muscle activity that interferes with your tone. This will free your tone and, consequently, free your ability to produce words easily and clearly.

Your body's neuromuscular system, however, has been programmed by years of poor singing habits to activate every muscle it can to help you control your voice. It will attempt to resist any changes in muscular coordination you try to make. For a while you may feel tension in the muscles under your jaw, in your neck, in the back of your mouth, and in your soft palate. These tensions are caused when the "wrong" muscles (your outer muscles) are reluctant to give up control to the "right" muscles (the muscles of your larynx) in producing tone.

Never work around these tensions by doing things like changing the position of your tongue and jaw, raising your soft palate, making more space in your throat, or changing the pronunciation of your words. You will only create other tensions. Just follow the instructions in the training program and do the exercises. Once you have successfully reprogrammed your neuromuscular system to accept your voice's functioning at your speech level, these tensions will disappear. You will then be able to sing with *release,* a condition in which your voice works without your having to *think* about it, or *do* anything to it.

Building Strength — All in Good Time

Don't be concerned about building a strong voice right away. The ability to increase the loudness of your tone will come by itself, after the coordination of your vocal muscles has been established. Once the "crutch" of depending on your outer muscles to help keep your vocal cords balanced with your breath flow is gone, your vocal cords will develop their own independent strength.

Little by little, your vocal cords will be able to hold back more and more air in the vibration process, eventually providing you all the dynamic (loudness) flexibility you'll need. In the meantime—or at any time, for that matter—you should sing only as loudly as you are able to stay on your speech level, with a clear, connected, and easily produced tone throughout your entire range.

I had heard about Seth Riggs's vocal technique from industry professionals for years. I bought his book and came to see him as soon as I could. Not only did the exercise warm-ups help me relieve vocal fatigue, but his assistance in applying it to my songs helped me maintain the same ease, control and power that I'd found in the exercise. I'm building more dependabilities in my voice by trying to sing more correctly. Thanks for making it easier, Seth.

Shirley Murdock

Singer
Los Angeles

What to Remember

Voice training:

1. *Develops coordination.* The first step in training your voice how to function at your speech level, is to condition your vocal cords to adjust with your breath flow without interference from your outer muscles. This frees your tone and, consequently, your ability to produce words easily and clearly.

2. *Builds strength.* Once you have conditioned your outer muscles not to participate in the production of your tone, your vocal cords gradually develop their own independent strength. This allows you to sing louder without your vocal cords needing any "outside" muscular assistance.

Practical Exercises

I studied with all the big retired Metropolitan star singers and repertoire coaches on the West Coast. *After two years of not getting into the semi-finals of the Metropolitan Western Regional auditions, I quit the competition (and further vocal study for a year). Then I came to Seth Riggs to study vocal technique. We had only 3 1/2 months to prepare for the Metropolitan Opera auditions. Seth said, "Let's not learn any new arias, let's rebalance the old ones." I entered the competition (over 2,000 singers from the 50 states). I won on the West Coast, went to New York City and won the finals there also. I flew to Zurich and won a two-year contract. Next, I signed a three-year contract at the Munich opera where I'm singing major lyric and lyrico spinto roles. Now, I am guesting at many of the finest European opera houses.*

It is exciting that the West Coast has such a marvelous vocal technique teacher available in the area. It always amuses me that old opera stars (and most academic never-was-beens) describe how they sang and call it vocal pedagogy.

What they fail to understand is that if a young singer doesn't have his teacher's particular vocal facilities, he can't sing like the teacher sang, thus vocal technique sessions become repertoire sessions.

Thank you, Seth. I could still be digging ditches and laying cinder block in Santa Barbara.

Eduardo Villa

Lyric Tenor
Munich

Caution

Please follow along with the material in the book and the accompanying CDs as my students and I demonstrate how each of the exercises should be done. It is important that you do each exercise correctly before you proceed to the next.

As valuable as the exercises in this book are for training your voice, *any* exercise can be overworked or misused to where it will do you more harm than good. You don't develop your voice by pushing it to its limit. You develop it by gradually conditioning it to work efficiently with a balanced coordination. IMPORTANT: You must **stop** doing *any* exercise whenever you begin to lose your speech-level posture, lose your connection from chest to head voice, or feel *any* strain or effort in production. Do not continue the exercises if you feel your voice is being damaged even slightly. See a doctor before proceeding. It is not necessary to go as high as the piano.

The exercises in this book will work best if you are relaxed—mentally as well as physically. Singers who have not yet achieved confidence in their instrument will often develop a nervous tension—a fear of failing to make a good sound. It is this fear, however, that sets up even more tension throughout your body, which in turn exerts more tension (the wrong kind of tension) *in* and *around* your larynx, which makes you more tense, and so on, creating a vicious cycle of fear and anxiety. There are ways to minimize this and other tensions.

As you practice the exercises be sure you:

1. **Maintain good physical posture.** Stand comfortably so you don't place stress on any part of your body. For example, don't slouch or lean on one leg. See page 86.

2. **Practice in as quiet an environment as possible.** Try to eliminate any surrounding noise.

3. **Keep a positive mental attitude.** These exercises really work. If you follow instructions, you will accomplish your goal.

4. **Stay relaxed.** Induce relaxation, if necessary, by deep breathing, and by doing any stretching or other exercises that promote blood circulation and eliminate nervous tension.

We have used a variety of different voices to demonstrate the exercises. Our purpose in using them is not to give you vocal models to copy but rather to demonstrate how each exercise should be practiced.

Part 1

BUILDING CONFIDENCE

Priscilla Baskerville as Aïda
Aïda—Metropolitan Opera
Drawing by Selene Fung © 1991
Used by Permission

You will begin your voice training by developing the confidence that it *is* possible to increase your vocal range to its full potential and to sing from the bottom to the top of your range without your voice jamming up, shifting in quality, or breaking. Some of the exercises are designed to directly bypass your neuromuscular reflexes—they won't work unless your outer muscles are completely relaxed. Some, on the other hand are designed to deliberately activate certain muscles in order to deactivate others, or to demonstrate an important concept.

Just keep in mind that all the exercises in this first part of the training program are only *temporary* devices to help you begin the process of freeing your voice and keeping it connected through your passage areas. They may sound somewhat peculiar to you, but that's part of what makes them work. You can rest assured that how you sing these exercises does not represent the way you will sound by the end of the training program.

I wanted to take this moment to thank you for helping my dream become a reality. Through your wonderful technique and teaching I was able to build a firm foundation upon which to grow.

Thank you for being there for me when I was experiencing difficulty in certain passages of music. After all, Aïda at the Met is no walk in the park.

Although I was some 3,000 miles away, you called or I called and we were able to solve what seemed to me to be "enormous problems." Then, on the phone, you reminded me of things you once taught me but I had forgotten. Suddenly those "enormous problems" were no more. You're a gem.

Priscilla Baskerville

Soprano
Metropolitan Opera Company
New York City

Seth was my fourteenth voice teacher. I came to him with a minor third "wobble" and never singing above a high F. After a couple of months, I was well into my head voice, and Seth suggested that I go into the Metropolitan Opera auditions. (Actually, he bet me $100 I could win it.) I was a pop singer and hadn't sung in foreign languages. In five more months (seven in all), I went into the '72 Metropolitan auditions. I came in second in the N.Y. finals, the only male finalist that year. (There were 2,000 applicants.) I sang opera in Belgium, France, Germany, Italy and Ireland for several years. I enjoyed singing opera, the big sounds, extended ranges and precise control, but I returned to my first love—musical theater.

Seth is an old time Bel Canto teacher, perhaps the first to extend Bel Canto into pop and musical comedy styles. I know his vocal approach works.

P.S. There have been three more of your students who have been National Metropolitan winners since my win in 1972. They are all singing in major houses in Europe and the United States.

Thomas McKinney

Baritone, New York City

Exercise Suggestions (1–4)

If you use too much air or anticipate the higher notes in Exercises 1 through 4, your outer muscles will activate thus stopping the movement of your lips and tongue. When this happens, bend forward as you approach the top notes of the problem exercise, returning to your standing position at its completion. Your concern about singing the higher notes will be lessened because the oncoming floor will make you think you're going "down" instead of "up." You can use this bending technique whenever you find yourself "tightening" or "reaching" for notes.

Problem note(s) sung at this point.

1   2   3   4   5

Exercise 1

Instructions: (Listen to CD)

Place your fingertips on your cheeks so that you pick up the weight of your skin from around your lips. Feel where your teeth come together. You push the skin in *that* far. This keeps the muscles relaxed so you don't feel you have to use a lot of air to move them.

Then, using an "UH" sound (*listen to CD*), let your lips "bubble" as loosely and as evenly as they can as you sing the exercise.

Let the air do the work. Just relax your lips as well as the rest of your face and throat muscles. The slower you can control the vibration speed of your lips, the better.

Don't worry too much about pitch accuracy at first. The relaxation and freedom of your lips, as well as the maintenance of a connected tone, are what's most important.

Try to do the entire exercise without "disconnecting" suddenly into a lighter production. (*Listen to CD.*)

Notes:

In Exercise 1 and in all your exercises, you must get used to the *transference of resonance sensation*. In the lower part of your range, your tone will appear to go straight out of your mouth, while, as you sing higher, into your head voice, your tone will appear to go more and more behind your soft palate. What you feel are the sound waves from your vocal cords activating those resonance spaces.

(Lip roll)

Approximate starting pitch:

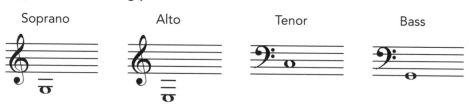

Practice log: Date started _____ Date accomplished_____

Exercise 2

Instructions: (Listen to CD)

Let your tongue lightly flutter as you make the same "UH" sound as you made in Exercise 1. The notes are the same. (*Listen to CD*). Remember, the object is to keep the tone connected as you sing into your head voice.

(Tongue trill)

Approximate starting pitch:

Practice log: Date started _____ Date accomplished_____

I first came to Seth when I was 19 years old. We connected my voice up to an E-flat above tenor high C, with no falsetto. Over the years, as I pursued a singing career, I began to use a lot of "throat gravel" for effect. It began to hurt the quality of my voice, so Seth gave me an alternative coordination and I'm back into vocal health.

Johnny Gill

Singer
Los Angeles

Exercise 3

Instructions: (Listen to CD)

The instructions for Exercise 3 are the same as for Exercise 1—only the skips between the notes are larger, covering a wider area of your range more quickly. Exercise 1 gave you a running start, so to speak, because the notes were closer together. In Exercise 3 the interfering outer muscles must let go even more. Your cords must be free enough to adjust to the wider skips.

Don't slide from one note to the next. Each note should be done clearly and cleanly. (*Listen to CD.*)

Sometimes it helps, whenever you sing from one note to another note that is higher in pitch, to approach the second note as if you were going to sing the same pitch *as* or *lower than* the one you are coming from. This helps to keep you from reaching.

(Lip roll)

Practice log: Date started _____ Date accomplished_____

Exercise 4

Instructions: (Listen to CD)

The instructions for Exercise 4 are the same as for Exercise 2. Again, only the notes and rhythms are different.

(Tongue trill)

Practice log: Date started _____ Date accomplished_____

Approximate starting pitch for Exercises 3 & 4:

Soprano   Alto   Tenor   Bass

In the Spanish-speaking countries, the Mariachi singers are the most numerous. The Spanish language, with the shallow 'ah' vowel, tends to pull the larynx upwards. Those two facts assist those of us who sing pop to belt too much. Seth got my larynx down and built a whole new middle voice with which I can sound like "chest," but not damage my voice or vocal energy in my concerts and recordings.

Daniela Romo

Singer
Mexico City

Exercise Suggestions (5, 6)

Once you can do the *lip rolls* and *tongue trills* with little effort, it will indicate that you aren't gripping your larynx with your outer muscles (it's hard to roll your lips or trill your tongue when the muscles controlling them are also trying to control your larynx to make pitch). It will also indicate that your cords are thinning and their vibrating length is "shortening" as you sing higher, and that you are using just the right amount of air to support their vibration.

The lip rolls and tongue trills, however, rely on the closing of your lips and tongue to help counteract any excess air pressure you may be using. Therefore, coordination of air and muscle can't yet be said to be taking place solely at the cord level. Developing the coordination that allows your cords to thin and shorten at your speech level (using just the muscles of your larynx to do the work) takes time. Unfortunately, your motivation can run out before you get to that point.

So, before you go any farther in the program, it's important that you get to *experience* the concept of cord thinning and shortening at the cord level—even if it means activating a few unwanted outer muscles to do it! We will do this in Exercises 5 through 11. *You must quickly abandon these exercises as soon as they serve their purpose!*

Exercises 5 and 6 are called *high larynx* exercises. They use the muscles above your larynx to pull it up. A raised larynx will stretch, and thus thin your vocal cords, making it possible for them to go into the shortened condition necessary to sing high pitches. But again, you are only using these muscles *temporarily*, just to demonstrate a concept. You don't want to use this technique when you sing. This is not yet speech-level tone production.

Over the years, I have studied on and off with voice teachers in the U.S. and Europe. Umberto Gatica, my engineer, had spoken to me about Seth Riggs. I began to work with him. For the first time in my vocal life, I discovered my "connected head voice." I began to sing tenor high C's and above. The new power, range and control was amazing. Thank you, Seth, for your assistance on Hombre Solo.

Julio Iglesias

Singer
Madrid

I first met Seth during the "In Living Color" series. Right away, the "balancing" of the "bridges" or "breaks" in the vocal range began. This technique holds you together vocally during extended recording schedules, and/or the tours to promote the album.

Jennifer Lopez

Actress, Singer, Dancer
New York, Los Angeles

Exercise 5

Instructions: (Listen to CD)

Don't jam the "nay nay" sound into your nose. It will be nasal enough with the exaggeration of the "n" sound.

Also, be careful not to reach up in chest voice.

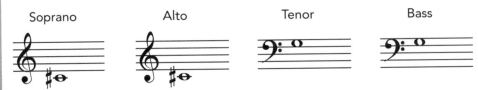

Approximate starting pitch:

Practice log: Date started _____ Date accomplished_____

Exercise 6

Instructions: (Listen to CD)

The instructions for Exercise 6 are the same as for Exercise 5—the notes and rhythms are different.

Approximate starting pitch:

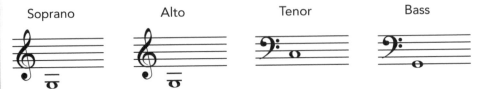

Practice log: Date started _____ Date accomplished_____

Exercise Suggestions (7–11)

Low-larynx exercises (Exercises 7 through 11) use the muscles below your larynx to pull it down. They also get your cords to thin and shorten. Yet, they do it with your larynx in a low position. It's lower than actual speech level, but it's closer to speech-level posture than the high-larynx coordination.

As you sing into your head voice, the feeling of thinning and shortening—if the exercises are done correctly—is similar to the high-larynx thinning and shortening. That is, you will experience a connected production of tone from chest into head voice. Yet, it's different enough so that you have to work through the connection all over again. Your cords will still thin and shorten as you sing higher, but this time without any assistance from the high-larynx muscles. In fact, the low-larynx exercises actually help deactivate your tendency to use your high-larynx muscles.

Just remember, if you *overuse* either the high-larynx or the low-larynx exercises, there is the danger that you will lock into one or the other of those extreme vocal postures, producing all your pitches off your speech level! So again, once you get yourself through the passage areas with a connected tone, you should discontinue Exercises 5 through 11. Exercises 1 through 4, however, can continue to be used. They make good warm-up exercises.

B renda Ritchie first brought me to study with Seth. I had heard of the "mix" and sometimes I got it right, but the exercises Seth used balanced the "mix" right away. Now I can sing a strong R & B "mix" up to B below soprano high C with no strain or lack of power. What a gift not to have to "break" into falsetto because my "mix" wouldn't sustain the pitch. Now I can use whichever qualities the song demands with no loss of control.

Tamia

Singer, Writer, Recording Artist
Tampa, Florida

*L*ike most natural singers, I had no knowledge of how to get from my chest into my "false" without a noticeable "break," or change in quality. As a pianist I had no trouble setting the key to hide my problem. When I joined Prince, the decision of keys was no longer up to me. Prince had worked with Seth and had sent Sheila E there too, so I was sent to him also. Hallelujah! Not only was the "break" mended quickly, but my style has become much better because I had more notes with which to riff.

Rosie Gaines

Singer
Los Angeles

Exercise 7

Instructions: (Listen to CD)

As you do 7-a through 7-e, put a little "cry" in your voice—but don't overdo it. (*Listen to CD.*)

This little cry slightly imposes your larynx down by activating the low larynx muscles, and deactivating the high larynx muscles.

But this "imposition" is only temporary. You want to cancel the tendency of your larynx to rise as you sing higher—the opposite of what you did in Exercises 5 and 6.

You will discard this low larynx "imposition" by the time you get to Part Two of the program, because you *never* want to force your larynx down when you sing, just as you never want to force it up.

When you do 7-a, make sure your soft palate stays very relaxed, with the sound going behind it more and more as you sing higher. And, make sure you continue to say "Mum" as you sing higher. Don't go to "Mam"— that would mean your larynx is starting to come up.

In Exercise 7-b through 7-e, don't take the exercise as high as you did with 7-a. The "G" sound (7-b through 7-d) and the "K" sound (7-e) are much more difficult to sing than the "Mum" sound because of the motion of your tongue. Only take them as high as is comfortable.

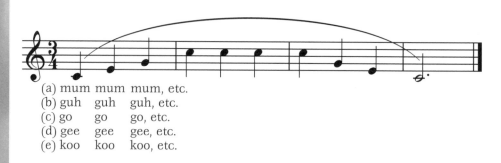

(a) mum mum mum, etc.
(b) guh guh guh, etc.
(c) go go go, etc.
(d) gee gee gee, etc.
(e) koo koo koo, etc.

Approximate starting pitch:

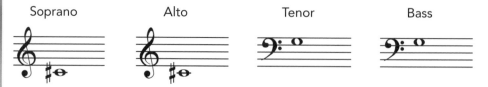

Soprano   Alto   Tenor   Bass

Practice log: Date started _____   Date accomplished_____

Exercise 8

Instructions: (Listen to CD)

The instructions for Exercise 8 are the same as they were for Exercise 7— only the notes and rhythms are different.

(a) mum mum mum, etc.
(b) guh guh guh, etc.
(c) go go go, etc.
(d) gee gee gee, etc.
(e) koo koo koo, etc.

Approximate starting pitch:

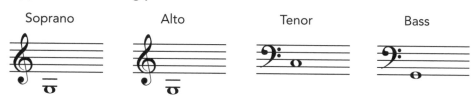

Soprano   Alto   Tenor   Bass

Practice log: Date started _____ Date accomplished_____

*L*ike all young singers, I want to get my voice together with as much strength, quality and control as I can. It seems to me that there is always some new style, new sound or new direction in popular music. I'd like to be ready for whatever happens. Working with Seth is building a vocal coordination which prepares me to meet all these challenges.

Madonna

Actress, Composer, Singer,
Dancer
Los Angeles

Exercise 9

Instructions: (Listen to CD)

As before, use a slightly imposed larynx as you do the exercise.

The higher you go, the "hootier" or more "hollow" sounding you should get to keep from grabbing. Don't worry if your tone sounds breathy or weak on the higher pitches. Just try to stay connected from the beginning of the exercise to the end of it.

Even though you are imposing your larynx down slightly, you must sing each vowel with the same pronunciation you would use if you were speaking it. For example, if you do the "Oh" sound incorrectly, it will "splat" as you take it higher. You've got to keep your larynx slightly imposed to keep it from raising. (*Listen to CD*.) You may want to think of singing "Oh" through "Oo" lips.

As you get into the upper part of your range, let your jaw drop just *slightly* to give the sound more space—but don't grab with it.

(a) Oo _____
(b) Oh _____
(c) Uh _____
(d) Ee _____
(e) Ah _____

Approximate starting pitch:

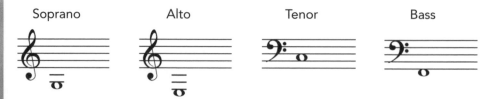

Soprano   Alto   Tenor   Bass

Practice log: Date started _____ Date accomplished _____

I began to study with Seth when I was 14 years old. We vocalized 3 1/2 octaves and evened all the "breaks." Today, some years later, we still vocalize and sustain nearly 3 1/2 octaves of vocal range and continue to strengthen the bridges.

Janet Jackson

Recording Artist, Singer
Los Angeles

Exercise 10

Instructions: (Listen to CD)

The instructions for Exercise 10 are the same as they were for Exercise 9—only the notes and rhythms are different.

- (a) Oo_____
- (b) Oh_____
- (c) Uh_____
- (d) Ee_____
- (e) Ah_____

Approximate starting pitch:

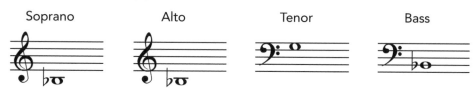

Practice log: Date started _____ Date accomplished_____

Notes:

Exercise 11

Instructions: (Listen to CD)

Still keep your tone a little breathy, as before.

The object of the larger skips between the notes is to increase your ability to release the tone. You have to let go of the pressure of one pitch so your cords can re-tune to the next one. But, don't release so much that you disconnect into falsetto. You must continue to connect your chest voice into your head voice. (*Listen to CD.*)

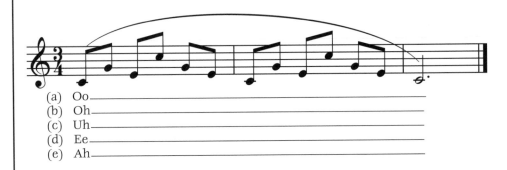

(a) Oo_____
(b) Oh_____
(c) Uh_____
(d) Ee_____
(e) Ah_____

Approximate starting pitch:

Soprano   Alto   Tenor   Bass

Practice log: Date started _____ Date accomplished_____

Notes:

Exercise Suggestions (12, 13)

Occasionally, an individual's voice is so "muscled up" that it is very difficult to get the cords to thin and shorten enough to achieve a connected sound from chest into head voice. When the exercises prescribed so far fail to accomplish the task, you may have to start with the "disconnected" condition of cord vibration, usually called *falsetto*. If you have already achieved a connection in your tone, you may skip Exercises 12 and 13, and proceed to Part Two.

The disconnected falsetto voice, like the connected head voice, lets you experience the freedom of singing in the higher part of your range without strain. But, unlike your head voice, *falsetto cannot blend with your chest voice* (thus the term "disconnected"). This, and the fact that it is impossible to increase intensity past a certain point, makes falsetto impractical to use, except for occasional special vocal effects. Falsetto, however, is easier for the untrained voice to sing. Because of this, it can be useful in leading you into the preferred connected condition of head voice.

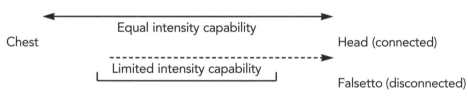

With all the activities one must weigh and balance in our wildly fluctuating business, there is never enough time to get your voice in shape. Singing seems to be the last thing to consider, when that recording gets started. It shouldn't be that way, but...I've always been able to maintain confidence that I can pull it together with my own personal application of a practical vocal warm-up. Thank you, Seth, and be cool!

Maurice White

Earth, Wind and Fire
Los Angeles

Exercise 12

Instructions: (Listen to CD)

Start with a falsetto sound. As you come down into your chest voice, try to make the transition as smooth as possible. Come down gently so you don't "fall" into it. Then try to bring in your chest voice more firmly each time you do the exercise. You want to replace your falsetto production, which can't blend, with head voice (which can).

As you do the exercise, don't panic when you feel the chest voice come in.

Come in lightly, till you feel it start to take—don't grab it in (*listen to CD*), and don't fall into it (*listen to CD*).

When you do 12-b, with the "Gee" sound, be careful. It's not as easy to start it as high as the "Wee" sound because of the activity of the tongue.

Remember, you may feel you are making your falsetto stronger—but you're not. Falsetto production merely gets you to relax in the higher part of your range so you can work on your head voice.

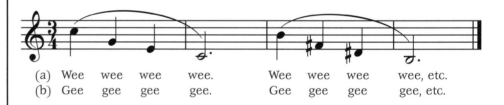

(a) Wee	wee	wee	wee.	Wee	wee	wee	wee, etc.
(b) Gee	gee	gee	gee.	Gee	gee	gee	gee, etc.

Approximate starting pitch:

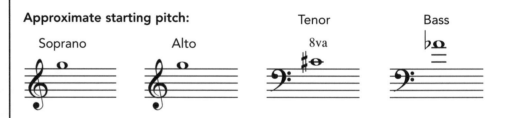

Practice log: Date started _____ Date accomplished_____

Exercise 13

Instructions: (Listen to CD)

You will now start in chest voice, go into your head voice and then back into chest voice.

And, again, don't take the "Gee" sound in 13-b as high as you do the "Wee" sound in 13-a.

Note: Once you can make a smooth transition from head to chest and chest to head voice, you may want to try Exercises 5 through 11 again.

(a) Wee wee wee, etc.
(b) Gee gee gee, etc.

Approximate starting pitch:

Soprano   Alto   Tenor   Bass

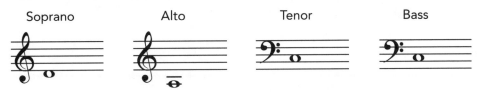

Practice log: Date started _____ Date accomplished_____

Notes:

I have had the pleasure of associating with Mr. Seth Riggs for the past 20 years. Seth is one of the most outstanding teachers of voice in the world today. He teaches the majority of pop singers that are among the world's most famous, as well as winners of the Metropolitan Opera Auditions in New York City who are singing in all the major opera houses in Europe and the United States. His understanding of the natural development of the singing voice is much needed today, with all the inept teachers who are helping to bring about the decline of the Operatic Voice. His book, Singing for the Stars, is one of the most outstanding treatises on voice production available today.

I was a member of the Metropolitan Opera for 14 years as one of their leading tenors, and for the last 28 years have served as Artist Teacher at Southern Methodist University in Dallas, Texas. I have studied voice with some of the greatest teachers of the past including Frank La Forge, Renato Bellini, Edna Forsythe and Della Hayward. They all stressed that "singing and speaking/speaking and singing" is one of the most important functions of the gifted singer. This is discussed throughout Seth Riggs's book. Since my tenure at Southern Methodist University, we have had some of the most outstanding teachers in the world giving Master Classes in voice, including Lily Pons, Evelyn Lear, Jerome Hines, Ramon Vinay and, of course, Seth Riggs. Mr. Riggs's book is used by many of our students and teachers with outstanding results, and I can only give the highest praise for Mr. Seth Riggs.

Thomas Hayward

Tenor
Professor of Voice and Opera
Dallas

I thank Seth for introducing me to a superb vocal technique, which functions in musical theater as well as the extended range demands of international operatic literature.

Angela Blasi

Lyric Soprano
Munich opera house
La Scala
Covent Garden
Vienna Staatsoper
Deutsche Grammaphon Recording Artist

Part 2
TOWARD SPEECH-LEVEL SINGING

So far, you have done exercises that let you experience singing with a connected tone over a wide range of pitches, without much concern about the overall quality of that tone or the way in which you achieved it. Each exercise served as a *mechanical assist,* that permitted your vocal cords to maintain a connection through your passage areas and, in so doing, became a *psychological assist* because it gave you confidence that you could accomplish that connection.

We will now proceed with exercises that condition your voice to work *only* at your speech level. This means from this point on we will *only* use exercises that bypass your neuromuscular reflexes completely. We will basically use what we call an unfinished or "edge" sound. This sound needs very little air and cord to work. Like the exercises used in Part One, the "edge" exercises will assist you in maintaining a connected tone through your passage areas—but this time, in a way that directly leads you into singing with a speech-level posture.

Your larynx won't raise or lower very much as your vocal cords make their adjustments, so you will experience a blending of resonance qualities. Also, your vocal cords will begin to relax, allowing you to sing even your lowest notes more easily.

When I was 13 years old, Quincy Jones suggested I work with Seth while I made my change from "boy soprano" to my adult voice. Most people advised me against studying voice during this difficult period.

Seth not only knew how to balance my unruly voice but, when I came out on the other side at 15 years old, my voice was easy and evenly together. What used to be the boy soprano was now a man's connected head voice with no strain. Thank you, Seth.

T.E.V.I.N. Campbell

Singer
Los Angeles

Notes:

Exercise 14

Instructions: (Listen to CD)

This is the first time in your program you are going to be doing an exercise that gives you the feeling of where speech-level sound is made.

Starting in chest voice, just below your break area, make a sound (with your lips closed) like a squeaky door hinge and inflect into your head voice. (*Listen to CD.*)

Be careful not to break into falsetto; you have to keep it connected. (*Listen to CD.*)

Mm

Practice log: Date started _____ Date accomplished_____

Exercise 15

Instructions: (Listen to CD)

Using the same squeaky door or "edge" sound you made in Exercise 14, start lower in the scale.

This time add a little "whimper" or "cry" to the sound to help keep the cords connected—but don't overdo it. You don't want to overcompress the air so use just enough to keep the connection as you sing higher. (*Listen to CD.*) More doesn't mean better in this instance.

The stopping and starting of the tone keeps re-establishing your tone at speech level so that you don't get off that level as you go through the exercise.

Once you can maintain a connection all the way through Exercise 15, go on to Exercise 16. At this time you may want to start monitoring any speech muscle activity by feeling the muscles under your jaw. These muscles should always be soft, with no tension whatsoever occurring when you do the exercise.* If there is any muscular tension, listen to the CD again to see if you have followed the instructions correctly.

Mm———————————————

Approximate starting pitch:

Soprano   Alto   Tenor   Bass

Practice log: Date started _____ Date accomplished_____

---

*This doesn't include transitional tensions that take place as you change vowels and consonants. It only refers to sustained tones.

Notes:

Notes:

Exercise 16

Instructions: (Listen to CD)

Exercise 16 is the same as Exercise 15, except you are reducing the number of times you stop the sound to re-establish your tone at speech level.

Mm

Approximate starting pitch:

| Soprano | Alto | Tenor | Bass |

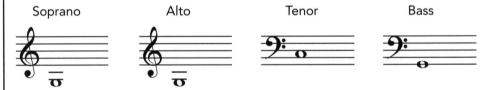

Practice log: Date started _____ Date accomplished_____

Exercise 17

Instructions: (Listen to CD)

This time you will take the edge sound straight through, only establishing your speech level at the beginning of the exercise.

Remember, you shouldn't feel any build-up of air pressure. It should stay even all the way up and all the way down. If too much air pressure starts to build, your voice will get stuck and you will start to "squeeze" your tone. You should feel as if you are using just a little piece of the cords—just the inside edges. As you learn to do it better, you can involve more and more air and cord as long as your outer muscles don't interfere. Keep checking under your jaw with your finger to make sure the swallowing muscles aren't tightening up.

Mm

Approximate starting pitch:

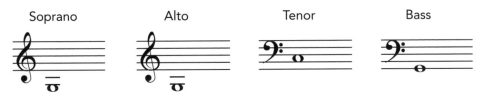

| Soprano | Alto | Tenor | Bass |

Practice log: Date started _____ Date accomplished_____

Notes:

Exercise 18

Instructions: (Listen to CD)

Still using the same edge sound—however, not as much—sustain the top note of the exercise.

When you get to the top note, be sure you don't prevent a natural vibrato from occurring. There is a danger of producing a "pinched" straight sound if you use too much cord tension (which demands too much breath pressure), or too much breath pressure (which demands too much cord tension).

Mm

Approximate starting pitch:

| Soprano | Alto | Tenor | Bass |

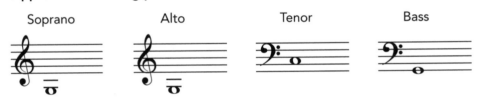

Practice log: Date started _____ Date accomplished_____

Exercise 19

Instructions: (Listen to CD)

Your neuromuscular system should now be convinced that your vocal cords can function without any interference from your outer muscles. Therefore, it's time to begin eliminating the edge sound, gradually allowing more air and more cord to become involved in the vibration process. Eventually you will reach a point of balance where your vocal cords can function efficiently and independently of your outer muscles without the assistance of the edge device.

Each time you do the following exercise, let your vocal cords relax more by substituting more air for the little edge sound. Take care not to disconnect the tone.

When you feel that your vocal cords have started to relax, go on to Exercise 20.

Approximate starting pitch:

Practice log: Date started _____ Date accomplished_____

Notes:

Exercise 20

Instructions: (Listen to CD)

Start with as little of the edge sound as you need to hold the connection.

As you sustain the top note of the exercise, open your lips slightly to form each vowel sound.

If your throat begins to tighten when you open to any of the vowel sounds, don't blast more air through. Instead, relax your cords by making your tone a little breathier. That is, don't make it so breathy that you lose the connection in your tone or have to enlist your outer muscles to force the connection to continue. *Remember to check the muscles under your jaw for tension.*

Don't be concerned that some vowels will be easier to sing than others. Just stay on your speech level and work on coordinating each vowel from that "home base."

When you have successfully completed Exercise 20, go on to Exercise 21, this time starting with the vowel sounds.

(a) Mm_____ Oo_____
(b) Mm_____ Oh_____
(c) Mm_____ Uh_____
(d) Mm_____ Ee_____
(e) Mm_____ Ah_____

Approximate starting pitch:

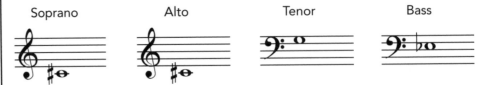

Soprano   Alto   Tenor   Bass

Practice log: Date started _____   Date accomplished_____

Exercise 21

Instructions: (Listen to CD)

Starting with each vowel, keep only the amount of edge sound you feel is necessary to maintain the connection in your tone.

Make sure that the vowels don't alter or "splat" as you sing higher.

When you stay on your speech level, your higher tones will have a softer, less intense feeling than will your lower tones. The lower tones will sound a lot brighter and stronger to you. However, what you feel isn't what the listener hears. The listener will hear a very free and clear sound when you sing into your head voice.

(a) Oo———————————————————
(b) Oh———————————————————
(c) Uh———————————————————
(d) Ee———————————————————
(e) Ah———————————————————

Approximate starting pitch:

Soprano   Alto   Tenor   Bass

Practice log: Date started _____ Date accomplished_____

Notes:

Exercise 22

Instructions: (Listen to CD)

Practice Exercise 22 until the edge sound, which originally led you into a connected speech-level condition, is completely eliminated. (*Listen to CD.*)

This may also be a good time for you to become aware of any excess body movement you may be using when you sing. Such facial motions as frowning, raising your chin, and so forth can only invite the participation of your outer muscles.

(a) Oo _____
(b) Oh _____
(c) Uh _____
(d) Ee _____
(e) Ah _____

Approximate starting pitch:

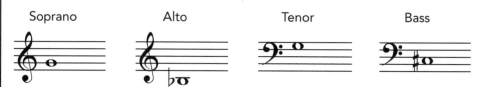

Soprano   Alto   Tenor   Bass

Practice log: Date started _____ Date accomplished _____

Notes:

Exercise 23

Instructions: (Listen to CD)

By now, you should be initiating and maintaining your tone with a relaxed speech-level posture anywhere in your range. Up to this point, though, all the exercises you've done have featured only single vowel sounds.

You also need to be able to maintain your speech-level production when a vowel changes to another vowel during a sustained tone. However, be sure you don't overproduce your vowels in the process.

Keep the same position in your mouth for the second vowel as you had for the first vowel moving your tongue and lips only slightly to change pronunciation.

(a)	Oo	Oh
(b)	Uh	Ah
(c)	Ee	Ay
(d)	Oh	Ah

Approximate starting pitch:

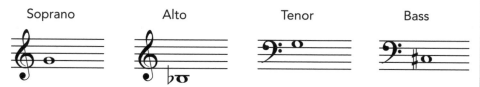

Soprano   Alto   Tenor   Bass

Practice log: Date started _____ Date accomplished _____

Exercise 24

Instructions: (Listen to CD)

This exercise continues the same idea as Exercise 23, only the number of vowels has been increased.

(a)	Oo_____	Oh	Ah_____
(b)	Ee_____	Oo	Uh_____
(c)	Oo (foot)_____	Uh	Ah_____

Approximate starting pitch:

Soprano   Alto   Tenor   Bass

Practice log: Date started _____ Date accomplished_____

Exercise 25

Instructions: (Listen to CD)

In Exercise 25, you are going to start in the middle of your first passage area, your main "break" area, which is usually the most difficult place you can begin a tone. You must learn to accept the split activation of sound waves, with half in your mouth and half behind your soft palate. Accomplishing Exercise 25 makes singing with speech-level production in this part of your range easy, because you get used to starting your tone in that "spot."

As you do this exercise, stay on the "headier" side of the pitch with a thinner piece of cord so you don't drop suddenly into your chest coordination. (*Listen to CD.*) Let your chest voice come in gently, by degrees. (*Listen to CD.*)

Don't be too concerned if the muscles under your jaw activate a little. They will begin to relax as you get more comfortable with the exercise.

(a)	Oo	Uh	Oo	Uh	Oo	Uh
(b)	Oo	Oh	Oo	Oh	Oo	Oh
(c)	Ee	Ay	Ee	Ay	Ee	Ay

Approximate starting pitch:

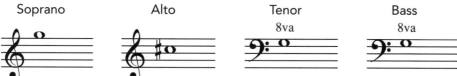

Soprano   Alto   Tenor   Bass

Practice log: Date started _____ Date accomplished_____

Notes:

Exercise 26

Instructions: (Listen to CD)

In Exercise 26, you will take every vowel individually through your range until, with each one, you get the greatest amount of tone with the least amount of effort. Remember, you must pronounce each vowel exactly as you would if you were speaking it. Nothing—absolutely nothing—should feel any different in your throat or mouth. Only then can you be sure you are singing with speech-level production.

(a) Ah———————————————————
(b) Ay———————————————————
(c) Ee———————————————————
(d) Oh———————————————————
(e) A (at)———————————————————
(f) Oo———————————————————
(g) Oo (foot)———————————————————

Approximate starting pitch:

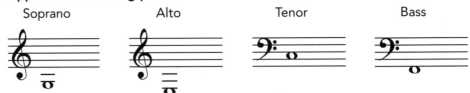

Soprano   Alto   Tenor   Bass

Practice log: Date started _____ Date accomplished_____

Notes:

Part 3

Technique Maintenance

You should now have a free, clear, flexible tone, with a blend of both upper and lower resonance qualities. It shouldn't matter where in your range you start your tone, because if you stay on your speech level, you should be able to just "talk on pitch."

However, bad habits die hard. As such, singing an actual song often becomes complicated when the inclusion of certain consonants, vowel combinations, and musical requirements threaten to disrupt your speech-level technique. When this happens, there are several things you can do to help you keep your speech-level production intact. You have done most of these already in some of the earlier exercises. Now we will do them with songs.

Notes:

Exercise 27

Instructions: (Listen to CD)

    Bend forward as you approach the problem note(s) of the song. This will help you break your anxiety about accomplishing that note. Remember to return to a standing position at the completion of the note(s).

Annie Laurie

Traditional

Max - well - ton braes   are   bon - nie   where

ear - ly falls the— dew.   And it's there   that An - nie

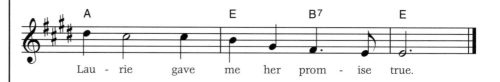

Lau - rie   gave   me   her   prom - ise   true.

Exercise 28

Instructions: (Listen to CD)

Use a little "cry" in your voice to discourage outer-muscle activation. However, only do this temporarily to "remind" your neuromuscular system that assistance from your outer muscles is unnecessary.

The Streets of Laredo

Traditional

As I——— walked out in the streets of La -

re - do, as I walked out in La - re - do one day;

I spied a young cow - boy wrapped up in white

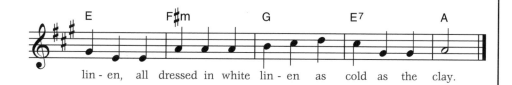

lin - en, all dressed in white lin - en as cold as the clay.

Notes:

Exercise 29

Instructions: (Listen to CD)

Sometimes it's hard to sing a certain note because the vowel you need to sing it with stays "anchored" to the lower part of your range. You can remedy this by starting with another vowel that, by its acoustical nature, makes it easier to sing that note without activating your outer muscles. After you use that vowel to start the problem note, you can substitute the original vowel for the temporary one, keeping it in the same "place."

If the problem vowel is:	Try:
a (as in "may")	ee (as in "we")
a (as in "cat")	eh (as in "let")
eh (as in "let")	ih (as in "sit")
ih (as in "sit")	ee (as in "we")
ah (as in "father")	uh (as in "mother")
uh (as in "mother")	oo (as in "foot")
oo (as in "foot")	oo (as in "toot")

House of the Rising Sun

Traditional

There is a house in New Or - leans they

call the Ris - ing Sun. It's been the ruin of

man - y a— man and oh, I'm on - ly one.

Notes:

Exercise 30

Instructions: (Listen to CD)

Finally, you can *sing the vocal line higher* than it's written. If you transpose the notes of your song higher, you will avoid getting locked into any one part of your range, and the problems that can arise from doing so. You may even want to do this occasionally with songs you aren't having any particular problem with, just to double check.

Shenandoah

Traditional

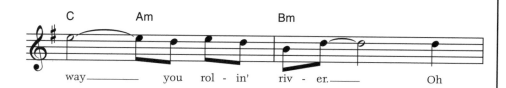

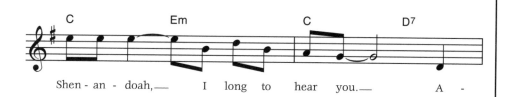

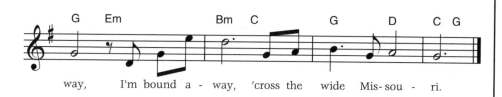

Generally speaking, if you remain sensitive to any excess pressure building up in your voice and do what's necessary to release that pressure, you will always promote and maintain a natural speech-level sound.

Notes:

THE AUTHOR SPEAKS OUT

The questions in the following section are the type which are most frequently asked of the author in his private lessons, as well as in his many lectures and master classes on vocal technique.

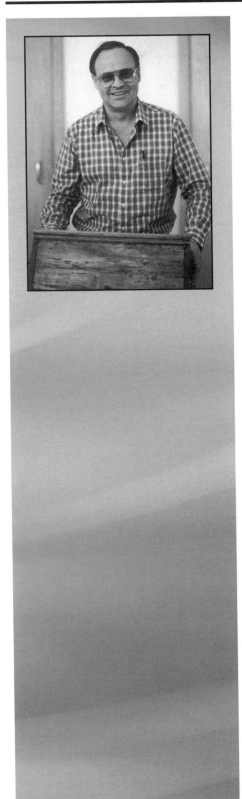

General Questions

How do you define singing?

Well, artistically speaking, singing is using your voice in a musical manner to communicate ideas and emotions to an audience. Technically, however, singing is nothing more than sustained speech over a greater pitch and dynamic range.

What is the key to singing well?

The ability to always maintain a speech-level production of tone—one that stays "connected" from one part of your range to another. You don't sing like you speak, but you need to keep the same comfortable, easily produced vocal posture you have when you speak, so you don't "reach up" for high notes or "press down" for low ones.

Is singing really that easy?

Yes. There's no great mystery involved. But although it's easy to understand, it takes time and patience to coordinate everything so that you can do it well.

Classifying Voices

How do you classify a singer's voice?

I don't! At least not right away. It's wrong to prematurely classify a voice before you really get to know what it can do. Too often, existing range is the sole determining factor in placing a singer into a certain category. The most important factor to consider is the *basic quality* of the voice. Assuming that your speaking voice is clear and unforced, your singing voice should be based on the quality of that speaking voice.

Range Extension

What do you expect the performing range of singers to be once they have studied with you?

Everyone has a different vocal ability, but, on the average:

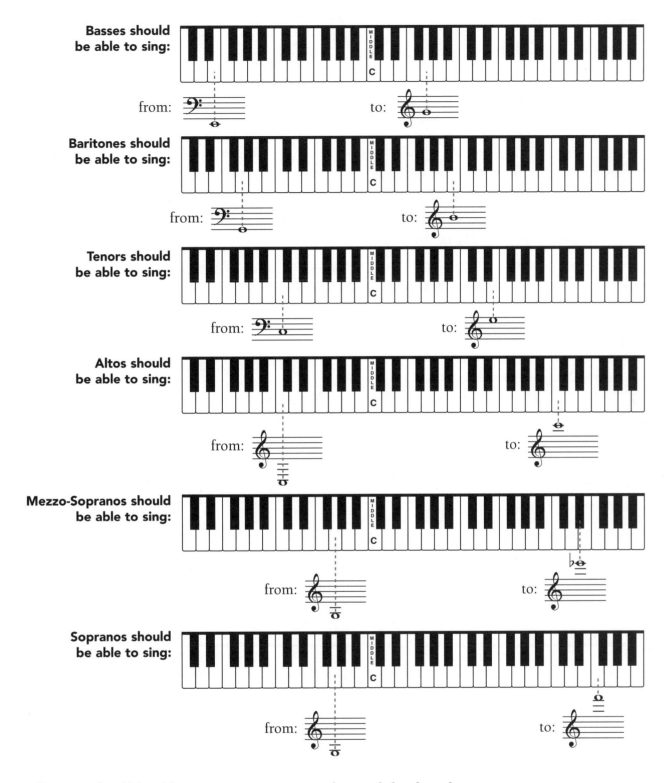

All voices should be able to maintain a connected, speech-level production of tone throughout their entire range.

Aren't those extremely high notes for voices in those classifications?

They shouldn't be if the larynx stays resting in a relaxed, stable speech-level position, allowing your vocal cords to adjust freely with your breath flow. Those pitches are well within the technical ability of a great many more people than you'd think. They may not sustain those notes constantly, but they should be able to sing them with good technique. This way they will always have a reserve of notes beyond the usual range requirements of any song they sing.

Tone Development

How do you determine what the tone quality of a singer's voice should be?

Again, I don't! A singer's tone should be determined by his or her own individual vocal anatomy and not a predetermined ideal held by a teacher—or the student, for that matter! It should be a blend of the top, middle, and bottom resonance qualities that results when the singer's larynx remains in a relaxed, stable position.

What about breathing? Doesn't correct breathing play an important part in your ability to produce good tone?

Of course. But the importance of breathing in singing has been overemphasized by voice teachers for too long a time. Correct breathing is a *by-product* of good technique—just like one's resonance quality is a by-product. You should never work directly at developing your breath unless you have a sloppy posture and a depressed rib cage (which collapses uncontrollably when you expel air). You indirectly develop the proper breath support for your tone as you condition your larynx not to move and your outer muscles to relax. When you use a speech-level approach to singing, everything, including how much air you use to move your cords, happens automatically.

My teacher says I must overdo my articulation when I sing, in order to make my tone clearer. What do you say?

Many singers assume that the reason their tone gets "muddy" is because their articulation is wrong. Consequently, they change or overdo their articulation. However, when you overdo your articulation because your tone is "muddy," all you get is well-articulated, but *still* "muddy," tone. You don't need to overdo your articulation if you maintain a speech-level production of tone.

What about using imagery to develop your tone?

Vocal imagery doesn't always work. Imagery that evokes a positive muscular response in one individual's voice may evoke a negative response in your voice. I prefer to use exercises that have a definite *cause and effect* relationship, producing a desired result, rather than relying on the nebulous descriptions of someone else's personal experience.

Is humming beneficial to developing tone?

Well, it depends on *how* you hum. Humming, if done correctly, can discourage many of the tone-manu- facturing devices that singers think they need to make sound. In fact, we use a form of humming in some of our own exercises.

Does cupping my ear help me hear my voice better?

No. It doesn't give you an accurate account of how you sound. You are just hearing amplified false quality from your cupped hand.

What is the difference between projection and shouting?

Projection is the acoustical phenomenon that occurs when you produce your tone with an efficient balance of air and muscle. Shouting, on the other hand, implies the usage of air "blast," which causes your voice to "jam up."

Using Microphones

Why should I bother so much about my tone quality if I'm going to be singing with a microphone?

Electronic amplification and alteration of your voice have an important place in the communication and entertainment media, but they must not be thought to replace healthy and efficient vocal production.

Singing in Different Styles

Do you have to change your tone production when you perform different moods and styles?

No! Most differences in singing styles are built into the music itself—the sequence of notes and certain conventions of singing that are popular during a particular place and time in history. When you adjust your voice to accomplish certain tonal "ideals," you run the risk of interfering with your speech-level tone production, which is very dangerous to your vocal health. Your voice can, however, be "colored by your mind." If you are thinking about what you are singing, there will be slight differences in your *delivery*, not in your basic production.

Singing Outdoors

Do you have to modify your production when you sing outdoors?

Not really. Singers should always use resonance sensation to govern their tone production. In this way, they can be consistent in their ability to sing no matter what the "enclosure" or lack of it.

Choosing a Teacher

How does one select a voice teacher?

First of all, you must be able to discern whether or not a teacher is primarily a voice technique teacher (one who shows you *how* to sing), or whether he/she is primarily a voice coach (one who shows you *what* to sing). Of the two types, the voice technique teacher is the most important, because without the technical ability to sing flexibly and clearly in all parts of your range, you are very limited to the material you can do.

For the initiated, a good voice technique teacher is hard to find. Many so-called voice teachers are just vocal "cheerleaders," who bang away at a piano while you follow along. That is not teaching you how to sing, however. You just get a lot of practice following a piano, and memorizing the notes of a song.

Furthermore, when the teacher's methodology consists mainly of using terms such as "give it more support," "sing from your diaphragm" and "open your mouth," you know you are in the wrong company. If you don't feel your voice improving in the areas of tone production and easily attainable range extension within a few weeks, you'd better find another teacher—fast!

Many teachers give their students the same vocal problems which killed their own careers and *made* them teachers. Before studying with a teacher, ask for a simple demonstration of the teacher's own ability—especially his/her ability to negotiate their own passage areas. Audition the teacher!

Is there anything else to look for in choosing a teacher?

Yes. Be wary of any voice teacher who just teaches his or her own sex, or just the opposite sex. If a teacher understands good singing technique, he/she can teach either sex, and at any age. Also, be careful of teachers who try to make you sound like *they* do or like they think you *should* sound. A voice teacher should only try to develop the vocal freedom that will bring out the special character of your own voice.

Should a voice teacher know how to play piano?

He or she should have as much piano facility as possible, but never—never—at the exclusion of a thorough knowledge of the voice. He/she should at least know how to play all the scales and exercises used for vocal training. However, be careful of the teacher who substitutes the plunking out of notes for knowledge of the voice. Anybody can say, "Sing this note." Few teachers, however, can show you how. It is unfortunate that piano skill often implies that a teacher has a more comprehensive knowledge of the voice than he/she really has. *Teaching songs is no substitute for vocal technique.*

Exploiting Student Voices

Many singers seem to have more trouble with their voices after they have been studying voice for a few years. Why is this?

In high schools and colleges, as well as in private voice studios, teachers often exploit the talent of their students. Without really teaching anything, *they* take bows for their students' own natural abilities. But, as you have already indicated in your question, some students aren't fortunate enough to survive the "training" received by these teachers. Students come away from their voice lessons thinking they are stupid when they can't seem to do what the teacher asks them to do. Actually, the teacher doesn't know what he or she is doing, and, if they do, he/she hasn't been able to communicate that knowledge to the student.

Voice Science

How about teachers who say they teach the "scientific" method of singing?

Many teachers in recent history have fallen victim to what has been erroneously termed "voice science." You see, any time you associate something with the word "science," it automatically assumes an aura of truth. That's very attractive to both teachers and students, who are anxious to grab onto *anything* that offers them hope of understanding what has unfortunately become a very confusing subject.

Of course your voice works, as does everything else, according to scientific principles. But those principles can be abused by those who aren't able to apply them. Prominent voice "scientists" have attempted for years to translate scientific findings into a useable vocal technique. They have made some remarkable observations as to what happens to voices during the process of singing. But that's all they are—*observations*.

Science, however, is not only knowledge derived from observation, but the skill resulting from that knowledge. In singing, that skill can only be developed through special exercises which balance your vocal coordination so that speech-level tone production is possible. The foremost vocal "scientist" I ever knew couldn't even sing in his head voice, and the part of his range where he did sing always sounded "dark," "throaty," and "wooden."

Then how does the "scientific" method work?

There are many variations. However, all have in common the manipulation of the muscles in and around the larynx by telling students to "open your throat" and "lower your tongue," etc. Some even go so far as to manually force the larynx into position, which is extremely dangerous, because permanent physical damage can result.

Shouldn't singers sing with an open throat, and a lowered tongue?

Yes, but that type of vocal posture is a *result* of good technique, not the *cause* of it. Imposing any kind of posture on a voice creates tension that can hinder the freedom of cord vibration, disrupt the balance of tone and make speaking words sound unnatural as well—even if what the teacher asks for sounds like a way to "free" the voice.

But I've heard a few singers who studied with teachers who use those methods. Why did they sound good?

It's very hard to know whether or not a singer already had a natural affinity for good vocal technique *before* his/her study with a teacher. Many voice teachers build their reputations around the successful singing of one or two students. Other people then go to that teacher because of the way those students sound, without knowing that those students would have sounded good *without* that teacher.

Performers as Teachers

Is it better to study with someone who has experienced success as a performer?

Not necessarily. A lot of people, and many educational institutions, have the mistaken notion that "star" performers have a wonderful ability to teach vocal technique. More often than not, however, a star's teaching method consists of a description of his or her own vocal ability. This is vocal death to a singer of lesser vocal ability and almost as bad for even a superior voice. Vocal stars can be excellent for teaching repertoire and stage techniques, but unless their own voices are balanced, and they know how to get the same balance in the voices of their students, they should be avoided.

It doesn't matter how many degrees a teacher has, or how successful he/she has been as a performer. A teacher needs to know how to get each of his students to sing through their range in a connected, easy manner, without any "breaks" or sudden changes of tone quality—again, speech-level singing.

Singing in Choir

Should your vocal technique be the same for choral (ensemble) singing as it is for solo singing?

Yes, you should always use the same vocal technique, whether you sing solo or in a group. However, choral directors sometimes want you to modify your tone (change the way you sing) in order to blend with the other singers in the group. This may be okay for those singers who have developed a solid vocal technique, but dangerous for those—the majority—who haven't. You blend, all right—but at what cost? A singer should never compromise correct speech-level technique.

Then how is a person able to blend with other singers and still use correct technique?

In order to blend with other singers, you must give your interpretive powers to the director, but only in matters of dynamics (within reason), diction, and phrasing. That is, everyone must sing with the same volume, pronounce words the same way, and begin and end together. However, no attempt should ever be made to "brighten" or "darken" the tone. Singers should always maintain a clear tone with a normal speech-like depth.

It's not the vocal technique itself that should be modified or restrained, but the *degree* of individual vocal expression put forth. If you're going to have good ensemble, nobody can be sticking out. A singer shouldn't want to stick out—that would destroy the concept of "ensemble."

What about vibrato management?

Now that's an interesting combination of words! Management implies that you're going to have to "manage" or "manipulate" your voice—to *do* something to it. Well, that's very dangerous. It's impossible to get a large group of singers to have the same number of undulations in their voices at the same time. Yet, it's also very dangerous to try to take the vibrato out—to sing straight, "flat" sounds. To do so, your cords must be pulled so tightly that there's no undulation in them at all. Choral directors really shouldn't be messing around in this area. A relaxed vibrato should exist whenever you dwell on a note long enough for vibrato to take place. It is a natural function of a free voice.

Are you saying that choral singing can be dangerous for the solo voice?

It can be, if the director isn't careful. Most choral singers tend to belt out notes in their chest voice, without ever going into head voice as they sing higher. This is death for the solo singer.

Is there a reason for the limited range development of choral singers?

Yes. Choral music is usually written so that each vocal part has a limited range. The basses never have to go any higher than maybe a D or an E natural at the most, right at the top of their chest register. The same goes for tenors, whose part rarely goes above an A or B-flat. Consequently, there's no effort to develop the upper part of their range. They never have to sing through their main passage area, which in a man's voice *begins* around D or E natural.

How about women's voices?

The same thing is true for women. It's a big deal if a soprano sings past an A or B-flat in most choral music. But, you see, right at that high B-flat is a critical passage area in her voice, where she goes into a sort of overdrive. You could call the area above that passage area a "super-head" voice. You have your chest register, and you have your middle register, which is in the head, but is definitely what you call a middle sound. You have your head voice, and then a "super-head," which comes in around B-flat. But you have to prepare for it early, by keeping your voice balanced up to that point, just as with the other passage areas in your voice. If you are singing in an ensemble and go "pounding away" up to A or B-flat, I can guarantee that you're going to ruin your high C and your D and E-flat in solo voice.

So this problem applies to all voices?

Yes. A singer has to be able to hear his own voice well enough to be able to progress through his passage areas in a balanced manner. A solo singer can hear himself during solos, but a singer in a group finds it almost impossible to do so. He keeps singing louder and louder to be able to hear himself. This encourages him to "grip" with his outer muscles, which prevents him from ever exploring the head voice area of his range. Singers with wide ranges shouldn't be as rare as they are. Careless singing simply discourages the upper range development of those voices.

Is choral or ensemble singing any good for the solo singer?

It's good for general musicianship. That includes following a conductor's direction, sight singing, and ear training. However, you could learn the same things as an instrumentalist, then transfer what you learn to singing. Aside from the development of musicianship, there is very little you can transfer from what you get out of choral singing into solo singing, unless the director knows what he is doing in terms of vocal technique.

Choir Directors as Voice Teachers

Why aren't more choir directors good voice teachers?

It has to do with the system that trains them. When you go to school to study to be a choir director—either undergraduate, or graduate—you are generally given the poorest voice teachers on the staff. Even if you have a good voice, the music department will figure that you don't need to have a solo voice. Yet, most choir directors will meet hundreds of singers every week, when they conduct. They will also give voice lessons on the side. Inevitably, they will pass along the same poor vocal technique they were taught, using terms like "support the tone," "place the tone further forward," or "sing from your diaphragm," without any real knowledge of what those things actually mean.

Popular Music and Traditional Teaching

Why has the attitude toward popular music been so negative in school?

One reason for the furrowed brows when mentioning popular music in some institutions is that many singers who record and make these songs popular have had no training at all. But that doesn't mean there is anything wrong with the music. A lot of it is marvelous. It's not all good, though, just like music written in any style is not *all* good. Traditional styles just happen to have had more time to screen out the bad material.

Another rarely admitted reason for the lack of attention to popular music is that most teachers, quite simply, can't teach it. Although basic vocal technique is, or should be, the same for all types of music, the stylistic requirements for popular music are beyond their own background as teachers. Interpretation of popular music is a very personal matter, with no hard-fast criterion for judging the successful performance of a song in that style. Tone quality and phrasing is determined by the singer. Often a teacher will avoid his lack of ability in this area by saying that the student should learn the "right way" first, and then sing the songs they want later, implying that any singing that isn't opera or lieder is a prostitution of the vocal art. Their usual methodology—badgering students about diction, breathing, tone color, posture, etc—which may be barely tolerated in the "classical" idiom, does not apply at all to popular styles such as country, rock, jazz, blues, and gospel.

Then what should they teach, if they can't teach those things?

Vocal technique! Just vocal technique! Teachers shouldn't substitute the peripheral aspects of style interpretation for basic vocal technique. It's a totally different thing. Most pop singing has one thing in common: it's on a conversational level. Opera and other forms of traditional styles are not always that way, but you must still be able to go into your head voice without leaving your speech level. Most students and teachers who sing opera base their modern idea of operatic tone on a concept of a "woofy," overproduced sound, which is dangerous to the health and longevity of the voice. What is interesting is that the best opera singers (of yesterday and today) sing in a clear, speech-level manner that lets you understand their words all the way through their ranges. This is the same ideal that people listen for in any type of good singing.

Selecting Music

When a singer first begins to study vocal technique, what type of material should he sing?

You should avoid any material that puts a great demand on your voice from a *dynamics* standpoint. Select songs that are more melodic, not those that need "punch" or require a "dramatic" dynamic level. As I've said already, singing songs is not vocal technique. Just because a teacher encourages you to "sing out," or gives you hints on how to interpret what you sing, does not mean you are learning vocal technique. Style and interpretation are no substitute for vocal technique. Without good vocal technique, style and interpretation are greatly restricted.

Singing in Foreign Languages

Should beginning voice students sing in foreign languages?

I believe singing in foreign languages gives a singer too much opportunity to sing incorrectly. The best way

to tell if a singer is singing correctly is to hear whether he or she is singing in a clear and unmanufactured manner. Very few people are able to tell if a foreign language is being sung correctly. If someone sings "Mary Had a Little Lamb" in a garbled manner, someone is sure to notice—but not if it's sung in a foreign language, where there can be a tendency to "overproduce" tone. A person should not sing in a foreign language unless he can sing in his own first.

Then why are so many songs in foreign languages required in schools?

One reason is that teachers in colleges and universities create work for themselves by encouraging recitals and concerts, promoting the same vocal literature *they* had to learn in school. Their students are usually being supported by their parents and the teachers are being supported by the school, so nobody is ever required to learn anything which would enable them to go out and earn a buck. You cannot earn money doing the art song repertoire that you learned in school, outside of school. No one is interested because, even if they understood the lyrics, the subject matter doesn't relate to them. Even when it does, the style or idiom often gets in the way of their understanding the words.

Is that the only reason?

No. Colleges and universities must meet certain standards in order to become accredited. You have to have so much French, German, or Italian literature memorized or you can't be graduated.

Why?

We've lived in the shadow of Western European-based art forms for so long that one is not considered learned or educated in the art of singing unless he or she can sing these forms of music in the original languages. It's really a ludicrous situation.

What can be done to change the situation?

Teachers should stop putting themselves in ivory towers and acting as if there were nothing else but opera, nothing else but musical theatre, or nothing else but popular music! A voice teacher must try to impress upon his pupils, actually insist, that they sing in an uncluttered, easy manner throughout their entire range—*and be able to sing anything!* Students must be given repertoire in all areas of vocal music, traditional *and* popular.

Practicing

How soon in my training program can I expect to sing high notes easily?

Immediately, since in our approach there is no strain involved in the production of tone anywhere in one's range. You must move quickly into the extreme ranges to ensure that you don't get locked in to any one part of your range.

What about teachers who say you should build your middle range before you try to extend it up or down?

That is a very popular, yet self-defeating philosophy. Singing in just the middle of your range keeps you anchored to your chest voice, with a slightly lighter approach maybe, but giving you no concept of how to get into your head voice. You must expose the "break" area (the most critical passage area in your voice) right away. Then, once you've established that it exists, you must proceed to eliminate it. This business of working on your middle range first is nonsense. With our speech-level approach to vocal technique, there is no inordinate pressure either up *or* down one's range. *All* your tones should be easily produced, and you should begin training your voice with that in mind right from the start.

What is a good dynamic level to practice?

Mezzo forte (medium loud) at the loudest. However, you must never forget *why* you practice exercises. You do so to set up the correct balance between your exhaled air and your vocal cords, allowing you to sing at a speech level, and to then have your neuromuscular system live with that balance. As far as volume goes, you should only sing as loudly as you are able to maintain your balance with a steady, normal vibrato. The intensity, or loudness, of that tone will come once the muscular coordination to produce pitches freely is established.

There doesn't seem to be a great deal of variation in the types of exercises that you use, compared to other books that contain vocal exercises. How do you explain this?

Who's to know if you are doing the other exercises with the proper balance in your voice? If just scales were all it took to establish a balanced voice, you wouldn't need a voice teacher. You could just sing scales all day.

The important thing isn't *what* you sing when you exercise, it's *how* you sing it. An exercise should help you connect your voice throughout your range—to negotiate the passage areas. Almost any exercise can be used, if you keep your voice balanced.

Exercises that require you to sing pure vowels *before* you have developed the coordination to sing them correctly, do absolutely nothing to condition your larynx to function independently from your outer muscles. As soon as you sense you are going to have trouble singing a note, your neuromuscular system activates those muscles, to try to *make* that note beautiful, or to somehow *fix* it.

Of course, you may be able to temporarily muscle your tone, but all you are really doing is reinforcing the same bad habits that got your voice into the strained condition it was previously in. You will have done *nothing* to train your voice. Your larynx should already exhibit a good deal of independence from your outer muscles *before* you begin to use pure vowel sounds. Otherwise, you will just "grip" and "squeeze" with your outer muscles as you sing higher.

Should I practice agility and velocity exercises?

Yes, but *only* when they can be done accurately with balanced tone production. It doesn't do you any good to plow through an exercise at a fast speed. Exercises should not be done quickly until you are able to sing each note clearly at a moderate speed, at your speech level. Otherwise, you only touch the notes so briefly that strained production is not detected.

How much should I practice?

You should practice as much as you perform, even more. They are not the same thing. Performance is the culmination of your vocal conditioning to meet the artistic demands you place on your voice for the purpose of communicating and projecting ideas and emotional experiences to your listener. Regular vocal practice keeps your voice aligned for efficient coordination, so that any temporary diversion from good technique can be recognized easily and corrected quickly.

When should I not practice singing?

Whenever you are indisposed with such things as a head cold, fatigue, etc., that could interfere with the physical sensations you use to judge your vocal coordination.

How often should I have a voice lesson?

That depends upon your ability and the demands of the particular music you are singing. A professional opera singer, for example, may have his or her technique checked by a teacher once or twice a week. For a beginner, though, or someone learning correct technique for the first time, I would say a minimum of two lessons a week, three days apart to start. Such a schedule should continue until the singer begins to grasp the fundamentals of the new technique. Depending upon the teacher and the student, this can take as little as one or two lessons.

A teacher shouldn't lead you by the hand every day unless you are both "crashing" on certain problems that need to be solved quickly because of professional commitments. Preferably, you should have time alone to make mistakes and work them out for yourself. Eventually you can wean yourself from your teacher.

You should only study regularly with a teacher until you are able to apply your technique to your songs. Then, all you need is an occasional check-up. Another pair of ears can be very valuable.

Singing in Rehearsals

Should you sing differently in rehearsal than you do in performance?

Yes, especially when learning something new. In rehearsals, all wise singers *save* their voices—not in the sense that you only have just so much to give, but to keep your voice relaxed during a potentially stressful situation. Rehearsals by nature are very demanding on a voice. It's stop-and-go as you learn notes, check pitches, work on blend, and everything else. This makes it very easy to fall back into old habits. Therefore, you should do what is called "marking" your music—singing lightly or even dropping the high notes down an octave, until all the notes are learned and you know what's expected of you. Once you know where you are going with your voice, your neuromuscular system will be much more cooperative in helping you sing the right notes with the proper technique.

Voice Competitions

What do you think about vocal competitions?

Competitions can provide scholarships, some prestige and national attention, and also an occasional beginning contract for performers. Yet, many of the world's best singers have never won a competition.

Decibel (volume) level, not a balanced vocal technique, seems to be the main criteria of the judges. Thus, lyric singers are passed over in favor of "blasters" who are headed toward vocal ruin. It has been my experience that most judges aren't good enough to have pupils in the very contests they are called upon to judge.

The Young Voice

How do you teach young voices, say under fifteen years of age?

For both boys and girls, basic musicianship should begin as soon as possible. A stringed instrument such as violin, viola or cello is good to learn. It gives the youngster a feeling of long, continuous, bowed lines, and a "vibratoed" quality of tone which is indeed similar to the singing voice. Piano and guitar are also very good as they will help in the later study of harmony and be useful as a means of self-accompaniment. Naturally, with all instruments, the involvement with reading music and rhythm is invaluable.

Then, as the voice becomes more responsive with age, the already activated musicianship supports and enhances the overall musical ability.

As far as actual voice training goes, however, one must be careful. In girls, it is not uncommon to find youngsters around ten years old who can vocalize easily from low G and A to E-flat above high C and above. And it is possible to maintain that marvelous start if those handling that voice are careful not to require any *heavy* singing. That is, competition in groups of older voices or participation in school musicals which require belting. These young voices will become fuller (rounded out), without loss of range, power, and quality, if care is taken to keep strain absent.

In male voices, the change from boy soprano to the beginnings of the adult male voice can be traumatic. It can happen dramatically (overnight in some cases), or hang in a "cracking limbo," bobbing back and forth within an octave range for a period of time. It is both embarrassing and bothersome, and indeed (if the young boy has experienced some success with a beautiful soprano voice) a horrifying experience. There is no promise that his voice will return in any consistent state of well-being.

This is a difficult period to live through, unless you have knowledgeable and patient vocal guidance from an expert voice technique teacher. The youngster must be monitored regularly to insure that he is keeping his voice coordination as balanced as possible through the change.